D0196726

"DID YOU EVER SEE AN APPLE TREE . . . a pear tree or a cherry tree out there in an orchard straining and grunting and groaning all over the place saying, 'I'm growing apples' or 'I'm growing pears' or 'I'm growing cherries'? No, of course you didn't. . . . the fruit just grows all by itself."

And we share the same ability, says Frances Gardner Hunter. She knows—and she proves— that the secret to an enriched and fulfilled life lies with a special and, with faith, simple formula:

"Hang loose with Jesus—let God do it!"

HANG LOOSE
WITH JESUS

Frances Gardner Hunter

WARNER PRESS ● Anderson, Indiana

HANG LOOSE WITH JESUS

A PORTAL BOOK
Published by Pyramid Publications for Warner Press, Inc.

Ninth printing September, 1973

Copyright © 1972 by Frances Gardner Hunter
All Rights Reserved

Printed in the United States of America

ISBN 0-87162-130-4

PORTAL BOOKS are published by Warner Press, Inc.
1200 East 5th Street, Anderson, Indiana 46011, U.S.A.

DEDICATED WITH TEARS
to those who sit within and without the church walls and live defeated lives.

CONTENTS

INTRODUCTION

You may have said, "What does she mean, 'Hang Loose with Jesus'?" when you saw the title of this book. I'll have to be honest with you and tell you this was not an original expression of mine, but one which communicated to me so vividly what Christianity really is, that I wanted to share not only the expression with you, but also what it really means.

In Miami, Florida, there is a friend of mine who gets burdened with all the people who try sooooooooo hard to be a Christian and who are miserable because they fail so badly and, like me, she's always running around trying to remind people to relax and let God do the work. She has quite a few years under her belt —someone told me around 85—but she's still going like a whirlwind.

Some of you may realize that as we get older we get sorta "flabby" in the underpart of the upper arm, especially when you lose a lot of weight, which she has in recent years. She always stands up, puts her arms out straight at her side, shakes them vigorously backward and forward, and says, "Hang loose with Jesus—get it?" If you'll just try that you'll get the idea immediately what it means to hang loose. Really, I could have said, "Let God do it," but I thought this sounded a lot more interesting.

Maybe if I asked you a simple little question you might understand better. What kind of a fruit tree grows in your own state? Think of the fruit it bears. Did you ever see an apple tree, a pear tree or a cherry tree out there in an orchard straining and grunting and groaning all over the place saying, "I'm growing apples" or "I'm growing pears" or "I'm growing cherries"?

No, of course you didn't. They just "hang loose with Jesus" and the fruit just grows all by itself (with little bit of watering and fertilizing, and so forth). But the tree doesn't work at all. I often think of Christians straining and grunting and groaning all over the place about how "hard" it is to live the Christian life, how hard they are trying to be a Christian, and my heart just aches for them. Because the secret lies in "hanging loose with Jesus" or letting God do it.

This book was written with a sincere heart that some of the fabulous little miracles that come my way every day may encourage you to "hang loose with Jesus" and let God perform more miracles in your life.

CHAPTER 1

IT HAPPENED!

I STOOD THERE, as immovable as a statue, because something was communicating with me that I didn't understand. I felt an unnatural power completely envelop my entire being. And all of a sudden I *knew* I wanted to be a Christian more than anything else in the whole world. For eight or nine months I had been investigating the claims of Christ and had been irresistibly drawn by the magnetic power of God himself.

All of a sudden a church was singing "Have Thine Own Way, Lord, Have Thine Own Way." When we got to the second line which says, "Mold me, make me," there was an overpowering awareness of Jesus Christ and I knew that Christ stood right there saying, "Here I am in person, Frances. Now what are you going to do with me?"

For months I had gone home after every church service having rejected the call of God's Holy Spirit, and every Sunday during mealtime we discussed over and over how it would be an impossible thing to go to the altar. I had seen people go to an altar and cry and at that time I thought they made a mess of themselves.

Even though I cried in the pew, I wasn't about to go up in front of all those people and make a spectacle of myself. But on this particular day I had an appointment with God, and there was no regard for what anyone thought of me—I wanted more than anything to be a child of God—and so with fists clenched behind me, and with all the fervency I possess, I pleaded: "God, *break* me—break me down to rock bottom if necessary, then mold me and make me into the woman you want me to be, because I want to be a child of God."

Then I was so afraid that God wouldn't take me that I went even a little further and said, "God, take my home, take my business"—and then I laid my most priceless possession on the line because I cried out, "Take even my children, God, but take ME—I want to be YOUR child." Somehow in that great moment of repentance and desire to be a Christian, God broke me into nothing. But I rose up a child of God! I've often thought later that God doesn't demand that we give up, but He does demand that we be *willing* to reject all for Him.

The word "repent" is heard little in churches these days—because it's old fashioned—and so many times "becoming a Christian" is merely a formality of signing your name to some kind of a slip, possibly taking a few lessons in doctrine, standing up in front of a congregation and "joining" a church. There is no regard to what the Bible says in connection with sin, another "nasty" word many churches just aren't using these days.

Somehow or other, we have become so blasé where the Bible is concerned we forget that there must be "godly sorrow" before God can really deal in a life. I am concerned about the number of individuals who are going to hell with their Bibles neatly tucked under their arms because they have "joined" a church, without regard to their personal salvation and without regard to a personal relationship with Jesus Christ.

In all of my church attendance and "belonging" to churches for the major portion of my first 49 years of life, I had never heard the word "repent" used, but today I certainly know what it means, and I think it's time we got back to that old-time religion which said, "Repent and be baptized every one of you" (Acts

2:38); "Repent ye therefore and be converted" (Acts 3:19); "Repent therefore of this thy wickedness" (Acts 8:22); "But now he commands all men everywhere to repent" (Acts 17:30).

When I think back even now of my own conversion and I remember the difficulties I had becoming a Christian, I'm reminded that the biggest stumbling block in my life was my refusal to admit that I had been a sinner, and without admitting sin, how could I possibly even think of "repenting"? According to my Bible, Romans 3:23 said, "All have sinned [except Frances Gardner Hunter] and come short of the glory of God." That false pride really made me suffer immeasurably, because Sunday after Sunday as God's Holy Spirit spoke to me about repentance I would not give in, and I would not bow to the fact that without repentance, salvation is impossible.

I began to read the Bible more and more, and as the truth was recorded in my mind, the sin of all of my indifference to God for the first 49 years of my life came into the recall pattern of my memory. There were many nights when I laid there sobbing my heart out in absolutely uncontrollable grief as repentance came into my heart, soul, mind and body.

I did not rummage through my mind to bring out the things necessary for repentance, but because I had saturated myself with God's word since I had a burning desire to be a Christian, God's Holy Spirit brought to my mind the things that called for repentance, to the extent that there were times in bed at night when I just sobbed and didn't even know the reason why, except maybe I just saw "me."

I'm concerned about "religion" in the world today. As I travel around and see so many different things operating under the name of "religion" I get sick at my stomach, and the more I see, the more I'm convinced we need to put aside a lot of man-conceived ideas and just "hang loose with Jesus."

Think of the exciting characters in the Bible and how they felt about Christ, and compare your feelings about him today. Do you have the same aliveness and zeal that they had? Do we feel a compulsion and a burden to share Christ with everyone we meet? Or have we gotten so sophisticated that we just forget to mention Christ for fear we'll be called a fanatic? I'm called that all the time and I just say, "Great! If you think I'm bad now, wait until next year."

Most of the time after I have spoken in a church, convention or club, people ask the chairman, "Is she real?" Let me answer that question for you: Yes, very emphatically I am real! They ask if I'm "real" because I don't talk about anything but Jesus Christ, because I don't think anything is worth talking about but Jesus Christ. And many people wonder how I got this way.

Did I just take that momentous trip to an altar (yes, I *did* go to an old-fashioned altar in a church) and then become on fire for the Lord? Did lights flash on and off—did the stars fall in line and march across the sky and did the angels sing that night? Did sky-rockets flash all over the firmament declaring that I had been born again and that I was a spiritual giant? Nope, such was not the case. And sometimes it wasn't easy, but the *desire* was there, and it seems to me that desire is probably the most important thing in becoming a growing Christian.

Jesus Christ is the most exciting man who ever lived! I make this statement every time I talk to a group, and it has recently dawned on me that there is a reason so many people don't believe this statement. So this book is written with a fervent desire that people and churches will "wake up" to the fact that it takes a personal relationship with Jesus Christ before

Christianity can become a reality and an exciting thing. Jesus Christ can *never* become exciting until you know him personally, and this means being willing to go back into the Bible to find out what a Christian really is and how we can all be exciting and excited Christians.

Romans 10:17 says, "Faith cometh by hearing, and hearing by the word of God." If you're really interested in that old-time faith, it's necessary to get into the Bible. I remember how fanatical I became about reading the Bible—I just devoured it in my early Christian days—and I remember vividly how I used to read the Bible when I went to the beauty parlor on Saturday morning.

As a new Christian, I was so afraid that people would think I was "religious" that even though the thirst had begun in my life for the living water, I still didn't want people to know about my avid reading of the Bible. So each Saturday morning I carefully covered my Bible with *Playboy* Magazine because I wanted everyone to think I was a real "swinger."

Somehow or other, as each week went on, and I had begun digging more and more into God's word, all of a sudden it wasn't important what the world thought about me, but it *was* important what God thought about me, so one day after I had returned from the beauty parlor, I met my pastor and said to him, "Today I was a real brazen hussy!" He was horrified, and said "What in the world did you do?" I said, "I took the *Playboy* Magazine cover off of my Bible in the beauty parlor, and couldn't help but flaunt the fact that I was reading God's Holy Word." What had really happened was that I had read in the Bible that if I denied Jesus Christ here he would say he knew me not when I got to heaven, and I certainly didn't want that. So I threw caution to the winds and in genuine repentance sorrowed over how I had covered up what I was reading.

The really exciting thing happened when I came out from under the dryer and two women asked me, "What version is that you're reading? We never saw anyone read the Bible with such interest." I told them it was my Revised Standard and they called the Bible store in the neighborhood to order one just like mine for each of them. This taught me an invaluable lesson—many people want to find an exciting Jesus Christ, but are stymied about what to do. Maybe this little clue will help you.

Each time I sit down to read the Bible I ask God to reveal some new truth in it just for me, and I would certainly recommend this to everyone. Just ask God's Holy Spirit to reveal the truths of the Bible to you, and He will. I don't believe I could understand anything in the Bible if I didn't ask God's Holy Spirit to tell me what it means. One night as I started to read the Bible, it seemed as if God wanted me to read in Galatians, so I started with the first chapter, first verse.

Now it's a peculiar thing, but for some reason or other in my Bible reading, God has never insisted that I read all the "greeting" part too attentively, but this particular night God indicated that I was to concentrate on the very first verse, and so I did, and in the RSV it reads, "Paul, an apostle—not from men nor through man, but through Jesus Christ and God the Father who raised him from the dead"—and all of a sudden that verse came alive to me because I almost jumped out of my skin as God's Holy Spirit revealed why I was to concentrate on that particular verse. I merely substituted my own name for Paul's, so in my Bible it now reads, "Frances, an apostle, not from men nor through man, *but through Jesus Christ* and *God the Father who raised her from the dead.*"

I dare you to put your own name in that verse

and see what a different meaning it has for you. All of a sudden *I* was transformed by the knowledge that I was an apostle, not because any man had said so, but because God himself had raised me from the dead through his son Jesus Christ, and I had been personally commissioned by God himself to be an apostle. And the same thing can happen to you. You yourself can become a divine thoroughfare for God's work.

Not only do we have to search the scriptures for the truth so that the light can really lead us, I'm also convinced that over and over again churches, people and even pastors forget to depend upon the power of God's Holy Spirit. We are told to be "filled with the Spirit" continuously (Ephesians 5:18).

The life that is not filled with God's Holy Spirit is a life that is useless to God. God cannot and will not use a person who does not appropriate the power of the Holy Spirit. And it is NOT a one-time thing. We are reminded to be *continuously* filled with the Holy Spirit. It is only when we are willing to surrender all of our life to God and willing to let His Holy Spirit direct every area of our lives that we can know the real excitement of the Christian Life.

Ask yourself if you're willing right now to do *anything* God calls you to do. How long has it been since you asked God to fill you with His Holy Spirit? Do you know beyond a shadow of a doubt that *at this moment* Jesus Christ is living his life in and through you and that you are filled with the Holy Spirit? If you can't answer that question positively, stop right now, and very simply ask God to fill you with His Spirit.

I hope you're not expecting something emotional or earth-shaking, because that's not what happens, but upon the promises of God's Holy Word, now that you've asked Him to fill you, thank Him right now for having filled you, and see what happens. And then, please, please, please *BELIEVE*.

I often ask congregations how many people believe the Bible is true—and rare is the person who ever says no. But do we really believe what the Bible says? If we did, we'd all be living a lot different lives than we do. We like to think that we believe the Bible, but if we really did, we'd all be willing to put our entire lives into a pair of nail-scarred hands and let Him control our every action.

"Old time"? Yes, but think of how the disciples depended on God's Holy Spirit. They were real "duds" before they were thrilled and filled with the Holy Spirit. Remember how these men had actually walked with Jesus, had eaten with him, had talked with him, had lived with him, had traveled with him, and yet they were certainly not sensational. Think about Peter, good old impetuous Peter. He was a *real* dud. Christ had asked him, "Lovest thou me?" and he said, "More than anything in the whole wide world!" And yet he denied Jesus three times—when he was really put to the test he said, "No, I don't know him. I don't know who he is!" That was the *great* Peter?

And think about the disciples who went up to the Garden of Gethsemane to pray with Jesus. Jesus left them after asking them to pray and went up a little higher in the garden. He came down and discovered to his dismay that they were sleeping. He woke them up and reminded them of their prayer vigil, went back up into the mountains a little higher, and when he returned, they were sacked out again. Three times he came down and three times they were asleep.

These are the great disciples? Really, these are like many of the people in the churches today, and maybe you're one of them. "Lovest thou me?" Jesus says to you, and you say, "Of course, I love you," and the next thing you know, you're asleep in the pew.

Then came that great day of pentecost when the promised "Comforter" would come and those in the upper room were filled with the Holy Spirit and Peter went right out and preached the Word and 3000 were converted. No longer was Peter a "dud"—he was a great man of God because he had been filled with the Holy Spirit. Look at the rest of the disciples—from that day on, they were true disciples. They zealously gave their lives for Christ after that momentous day, and zealousness is what it takes to have an exciting Christian life. Dedication to Christ—and total surrender.

God certainly doesn't call all of us to do the same things. In my case He put a very special call on my life and because of His call and my response, many fabulous and exciting things have happened which I want to share with you. It's because I am always "hanging loose with Jesus" that allows these things to happen.

CHAPTER 2

ARE YOU AWARE?

Of Your Needs?

RECENTLY I WAS privileged to be the speaker at a state penitentiary for women. This was the first time I had ever spoken at a penitentiary. I made a few mental notes and we entered the prison. It all looked so simple—we just walked up the steps to the gate and as if by magic it opened (of course there was a television "eye" watching us and since we were expected, the door magically opened) and we went in.

It was a beautiful day, but somehow, just as quickly as the door had opened, it clicked shut with an ominous sound, and in spite of the sunshine, a chill went through my entire body. My husband and my daughter had accompanied me on this trip, and we all glanced at each other when we heard that odd little sound that separates a person from freedom until a "freedom button" is pushed to let you out.

The warden met us and very graciously escorted us to the chapel. I had just come from a lunchtime talk at a Christian woman's club, I was slightly late and running behind schedule (as usual) and didn't have time for any briefing as we flew down the corridor. I hadn't had much time to think about how I should talk to these women and had no briefing at all, but I thought it might help me if I knew what the nature of their offenses was, so I casually asked, "What are most of these women in here for?" thinking that the worst charge would probably be shoplifting, vagrancy or the like.

I was not prepared for the answer which came back when she looked at me and said very seriously, "Murder . . ." and before she could say another word I slowed down and said, "Are you kidding?" and she said very simply, "These are the hardcore criminals of the state." I think for a moment my heart sank. I could see me sashaying right into a roomful of murderesses and the like and telling them about how much God loves them and how sweet Jesus is and I could see them rioting or something to that effect, so as I walked up to the podium to speak, I really cried out for God to do the talking for me, and this is what resulted just by relying on God.

I very simply gave the testimony of my life, telling the women that I did not become a Christian until I was 49 years of age, and then when I found Christ in such an exciting way He had transformed my life completely. I stood there and looked at the searching faces and I wondered which one of them was a murderess or which *ones* were the murderesses or which one had been a junkie, and would you believe I couldn't tell a thing about any of them. All I knew was that as I looked at them, they were all souls to me.

They were women whose lives had been misdirected somehow or other, but women whose souls were just as precious to God as mine. I thought of how I could possibly tell them that God could transform their lives through Jesus Christ. I knew I couldn't promise them that the doors of the jail would open and they would all miraculously be pardoned, because there is a price that we pay for sin and the price must be paid, so I really screamed for God to put the words in my mouth—to fill me with His Holy Spirit so completely that not a single word of mine would come out, but only His.

Then I very simply told them that even if they had to spend the rest of their natural lives in jail paying for a crime they had committed, God could forgive them of their sins and give them a peace in their lives that nothing else could, and that they could find a joy in life and a contentment that NOTHING else in the whole wide world would bring. I also told them that sin was sin in God's eyes, and that we all had to admit that we were sinners because the Bible says, "All have sinned and come short of the glory of God," and then I told them they didn't need to think that their sin was any bigger than mine, because since sin is sin, I had been as guilty as they; the only thing was that my sin was probably of a different nature than theirs, but in God's eyes it was all the same.

After I had spoken—and believe me, the whole time I was speaking, I was fervently praying for God's Holy Spirit to envelop the entire jail because my heart was crying out for the needs of these women—I very simply asked them if they would like to have their lives transformed and if so, to pray a very simple little prayer just asking God to forgive their sins. I assured them that if they were sincere, God would forgive them in the twinkling of an eye, and after they had asked forgiveness, just to ask Christ to come into their hearts and take control of the throne of their lives. Then I told them if they didn't know how to pray, that I would pray a little prayer out loud, and they could silently pray this little prayer after me.

I started the sinner's prayer softly and pleadingly —"Lord Jesus, forgive my sins"—and then allow them time to pray these words silently. But God's Holy Spirit had so completely enveloped and engulfed that entire chapel that all of a sudden I heard the most beautiful sound in the world—the voices of these inmates joined together, sobs interrupting their words, tears streaming down their faces, praying *out loud*, asking God to forgive them, and asking Christ to come into their hearts. The tears that flowed that day could have been called the River of Repentance as these women begged God to forgive them.

I don't know if I have ever felt the power and presence of God's Holy Spirit like I did this day. As we left, I ran down and shook hands with each woman there, then as my tearful husband and child came over to me, I said to my 16-year-old daughter, "Joanie, what in the world caused such a tremendous response?" And a 16-year-old gave me a fabulous reply. She said, "Mother, they were *aware* of their needs, and most of the people who sit in churches today are not aware that they need a personal relationship with Christ!"

We made a short tour of the prison, but even that was in hushed tones, because we were so keenly aware that we had truly been with God in that jail. We walked back to the front gate, the freedom button was pushed and we re-entered the world outside, but I couldn't help but wonder how many of the women on the inside of that jail were now more *free* than many of the people who look free on the outside.

Of Your Responsibility?

I'm often amazed at the ability of young children to understand the message and the urgency of the gospel. I was conducting a soul-winning class with a church one night and the pastor's 10-year-old son was present as I was instructing the class how to use the Four Spiritual Law booklets. I always explain the necessity of asking God's Holy Spirit to prepare a heart, and then asking God to fill the person going out to share the booklet with His Holy Spirit so that what God wants said will be said and nothing else.

So many people have a real fear of sharing Christ with other people, so as a little trick to arouse their interest at the end, I always kid them by saying that the little booklets cost 25 dollars each; then a big gasp comes out, and I hasten to assure them that if they will use the book and share Christ with someone during the next week the books are donated by me and are absolutely *free*.

I hadn't really thought about the 10-year-old paying much attention to me, but I didn't understand the sincerity of his heart concerning his own commitment to Christ, nor the seriousness of his desire to share Christ with some of his friends. The next day when he came home from school he was jubilant and he couldn't wait to tell me what happened.

He had taken the little booklet to school, but he didn't have time to read the entire thing to the friend he had prayed for, so he just pointed to the two circles which indicates a Christian and a non-Christian life and said, "Which one is you—the messy one or the

good one?" and his friend replied, "The messy one."
They my friend said, "Would you like to have the other
kind of life?" His friend replied in the affirmative, so he
simply said, "Well, just pray this prayer and ask Jesus
to come into your heart, and you'll have the other kind
of life."

His friend prayed the prayer. Now, my first question
to a new convert is, "Where is Christ right now?" to be
sure they know Christ is in their heart, and the boy
remembered I asked them something, but couldn't remember what, so he simply said, "How do you feel?"
And his friend said, "Joyful."

I relate this story because this decision may or may
not last a lifetime, but it's a start in the life of a young
boy. Most important, a 10-year-old boy is *aware* of his
responsibility as a Christian and is *aware* of the needs
of his friends. Wouldn't it be fabulous if we were all
aware of the needs of all of our friends?

CHAPTER 3

DAY-BY-DAY

God on the Spot

EVERY SO OFTEN my "prayer power" is really put on
the line by individuals. After my first service at a
state camp meeting, a number of ministers and lay-
men came up to me and said, "Frances, will you pray
one of your 'dumb' prayers for us?" Without a moment's hesitation, I replied, "Certainly!"

Then they told me the following story: They had
drilled a well during the past week and had hit beautiful spring water, but a rock had been sucked up into
the pipe which was down 276 feet, and the water was
shut off as a result. Two days of intensive working to

get the rock out was to no avail. The well-digging company was coming the next day to take the pipe up, remove the rock and sink the pipe again at a tremendous expense. They asked me to pray and ask God to remove the rock.

Inwardly I think I groaned as I said, "Lord, they really put my faith on the spot, don't they?" And I had no more than said this when I realized they weren't putting me on the spot at all, they were putting God on the spot. At this moment the paraphrased scripture in Malachi came to my mind: "Try me, test me, prove me, and I will open the windows of Heaven and shower down blessings far greater than you can contain," and that's just exactly what I did.

A large circle had formed for the prayer, and I made a firm statement. "If there is anyone in this circle who doesn't believe that God can get that rock out of there, *get out of the circle*, because I don't want any unbelievers in it." Some stepped out, and when the circle was re-formed, I merely prayed this simple little prayer: "God, this is your money. You can spend it to have the pipe taken up and put down again, or you can use it to win souls to Jesus Christ by merely getting the rock out. I don't know how you're going to do it, Lord, but thank you anyway."

Right now I'm wondering if I even believed it myself. There are times when I pray automatically because this is what I *know* God wants me to do, and I don't believe I even think at the moment as to whether or not He will do it, I only know that His Holy Spirit has told me to pray.

Just then a pastor came up and asked me to go and pray for an individual with multiple sclerosis, and while I was walking to the car, I heard a mighty shout go up—they had turned the pump on, and the water was shooting out like a fire hose! *No more rock!*

The fabulous thing about God is we never really

understand how He works—we just know that He does!

Would God Do It For Me?

It's amazing how miniature our faith is at times—and it's amazing what God will do for us if we will just believe and trust!

I started driving from Anderson, Indiana, to Lafayette to speak at Purdue University at about 10 A.M. on a foggy, rainy day. As I drove along, it was almost impossible to see the road or the cars in front, and the only thing that made it possible to see the oncoming cars was their headlights. The fog kept getting worse and worse until I was just crawling along at about 15 miles an hour. The windshield wipers were going full speed, but they still failed to keep the water off the windshield.

After I had gone over three sections of the highway which were covered with water, I began to panic and decided I had better find a gas station and call my husband who was auditing in Anderson to see if he felt I should come back. Then I said to myself, "That's silly, Charles isn't the one to ask, God is," so I said, "Lord, shall I turn around and go back?" Then I believe the devil got in the car with me and said, "Look, there won't be anyone coming out in Lafayette to hear you in such bad weather. Why don't you go back?"

However, I sure couldn't hear God speaking to me, so I continued. After another three or four miles, I really began to panic because it was almost impossible to drive. I desperately looked around for a little patch of blue in the sky when I stopped to fill up with gasoline, and couldn't see one tiny little spot that looked promising. I got back into the car and started on and began thinking to myself (or should I say to God?).

My conversation went something like this: "God, you couldn't stop the rain and turn the sky blue, could you?" I looked around again for a little sign of blue sky, but none! Then I continued "thinking to God," and I said "Now, Lord, I KNOW you could, because the Bible says you parted the Red Sea, and if you could part the Red Sea, and I know that you did, then I know that you could stop this rain and turn the sky blue."

Then the devil got in the car again (maybe he never got out) and said, "Well, sure he could turn the sky blue and stop the rain, but why should He do that for you? Who are *you*?" And I thought, "That's right, who am I to ask God for something like this?" Then another thought came into my mind . . . "Who am I? I'm God's girl—I'm a child of God and because I am God's girl, the Bible says I can ask for whatever I want, and it will be done!" (Matthew 21:22).

So very simply I said, "God, you know I can't see well enough to get through this rain, so would you please stop the rain and make the sky blue?" God's word says to trust Him, and that's all I did, but believe it or not, within 30 seconds the rain stopped, and within one minute the sky was blue and I drove all the way to Lafayette on dry highways and under blue skies. When I arrived at the university they asked me if I had noticed the tremendous change in the weather, and I related the story to them.

As I have retold this story in the area where it happened, I have always said, "Maybe you won't believe that God would be willing to do this for me, but I believe He loves me enough to do this for me, just like He loves *you* enough to do it for you, if you will only ask!" And in each service someone has come up to the microphone to tell the audience that they vividly remember the rain stopping and the sun coming out so suddenly on this particular Thursday. I think it's fabulous how God always lets someone else see the miracles, too!

This story thrills me so much because it brings to mind the fact that God is still in the miracle-making business today just as He was when He stopped the prayer of one man. Joshua wasn't afraid to ask for the sun, moon and stars for about 24 hours because of the glory of God, so let's all start asking more!

Jesus Christ Overlays My Signature

"So don't be anxious about tomorrow. God will take care of your tomorrow, too. Live one day at a time."
(MATT. 6:34, LNT)*

One of the most exciting stories I know concerns my husband and one of the things he did before I ever met him. Sometime in 1968, God indicated to him that he was to cut his production to half time. Charles is a partner in a C.P.A. firm and so without any hesitation whatsoever, he went to his partners and told them what God had indicated. He then very systematically went to his clients, or spoke to them as he was working for them, telling them what God had told him to do, and explaining that if they were sent new young men to do the work, Charles would still be there to do the overall supervisory work necessary. Some of them asked, "What are you going to be doing with the other half of your time?" To which Charles had to reply honestly that he didn't know because God hadn't revealed that to him yet.

With nothing more than trust in God and the knowledge that God himself was the one who advised him to cut down to half production, Charles continued, and still did not know what God wanted out of his other half time. There was no questioning on his part, because he knew that God, in His perfect tim-

*From *The Living Bible*, © 1971 Tyndale House Publishers, Wheaton, Illinois. Used by permission.

ing, would reveal to him exactly what he was to do. Charles began interviewing new men with the idea of replacing himself for the half time when he knew he would be out doing the Lord's special work, and one by one outstanding young men came to work for the firm.

Charles still didn't know what the Lord wanted, and then all of a sudden the Lord made our paths cross, and after running to keep up with God in our courtship, we were married. Then it became clear to Charles why God had wanted him to get his business affairs reduced to give him more time, because he was to spend half his time traveling with me on tour. The thing that I think is so amazing and thrilling about this story is that Charles did not demand to know what God wanted with the rest of his time, nor did he question God and say, "Lord, how can I support myself working half time?" He only knew that he had to be obedient to God and in being obedient to God he again proved that God is the God of miracles.

Charles called me yesterday to tell me what information the computer had come up with for the last fiscal year of the company. If you work 40 hours a week, that's a total of 2000 hours per year. The computer came back and told Charles that he had worked exactly 1025 "billable" hours during the last fiscal year, just exactly as God had told him to.

As Charles interviews applicants for his company, each applicant is told, "God is putting together a firm, and if He wants you in it, there's no way for you not to become a part, but if God doesn't want you in it, there's no way you can get in." And the interesting thing is how God has brought outstanding young men into the company.

One of the newest additions to the company accompanied us on an audit of a Midwest college. It was a tremendous audit and very time consuming, and at times an audit can be frustrating if all things don't go together the way they should. When we started, we had prayed and asked God to see that those working had the knowledge and wisdom to see that the audit was completed to everyone's satisfaction within five-and-a-half days. The audit started Monday morning, and we had to leave the college by 2:30 the next Saturday afternoon, which meant the audit had to be completed by 2 P.M. to give us time to get our suitcases in the car and be ready to leave for the airport. The new auditor said it just couldn't be done!

They worked hard and long. Let me explain right here and now that many people think you can ask God to do the work for you, but that's a misconception. Charles had prayed and asked God to give them the ability to finish the audit, but he didn't just say, "God, I want to work five hours a day—you do the rest!" No, he did not. They worked hard and long hours.

On Thursday as we were eating dinner the new auditor said, "We'll never make it—we can't do a satisfactory job and be out of here by Saturday." Charles calmly said, "Oh, yes, we will, because we prayed." Saturday morning Charles got up bright and early to get to the college at the crack of dawn because they were really going down to the wire, and as he walked to the building where he was conducting the audit, he realized he only had a key to the inside office and not the outside building, so he prayed and said, "Lord, you know how much we've still got to do to get that audit finished, so will you see that someone gets there to open the outside door for me?" And then he added, "Thank you very much!"

As he walked around the corner to the building, a guard from the inside opened the door and let him in. He didn't even waste time opening the door! God knew how precious time was on this last day. Everyone worked fast and furious, and all of a sudden the young auditor put the last report in his briefcase. Charles looked at him and said, "Are you satisfied with the thoroughness of the audit?" He said, "Yes, I sure am!" Charles said, "What time is it?" The young man grinned as he looked at his watch. God had taken them right down to the wire—it was exactly 2:00 P.M.!

You may have noticed that I have emphasized throughout this story that everyone had to be satisfied with the audit. Many times people will short-cut things to get them done on time, but I like my husband's theory on this. He says, "When I put my signature on a tax return or on an audit, Jesus Christ overlays my signature and it has to be done right!" Think of the real responsibility that every Christian has as he does his work—remembering that Jesus Christ is overlaying his signature. Isn't that an awesome thought? But a thrilling one, to say the least.

Not All Experiences Are Mine!

I like to share letters from people who write to me what God has done for them.

Dear Frances,

I just must share with you the marvelous way God has answered prayer.

I had felt I just couldn't go through life alone and had prayed the last two months for God to please not let me live. Isn't that awful! After reading your book, *Hot Line to Heaven*, I promised God to put my whole life on the altar. I said: "Lord, if you have a purpose for my life I need to know." We'd been discussing "fleeces." I said, "Will you cause a meeting of a small group to be held while Frances is in our town? At that meeting will you let me know your plan for my life by having Frances say, directly to me, one of two things, 'God has a work for you to do alone' or 'God will send you a husband.' " I didn't tell anyone what the fleece was because I wanted God to be the influence. All day Wednesday the devil kept saying, "That meeting is for couples, you'll feel out of place." Then he said, "What if the answer is 'God wants you alone,' " but I had put that on the altar when I said "Take it all." While you prayed at midnight Wednesday, the devil said to me, "You didn't get a message *at all!*" and I said "Lord, please speak to me!"

I don't know if you even remember and doubt if anyone else really paid much attention, but when you finished praying you spoke a sentence to the couples then pointed to me and said, "You watch out, the Lord is going to send you a husband!" The thing that excites me most is that God did, step by step, just as I asked of him: (1) called the meeting, (2) caused you to speak; (3) directly to me; (4) in almost the exact words I had used. I think I'd be just as excited had He used the other phrase—but I know this was His answer. And the strange thing is the anxiety is gone and I believe I can wait 10 years if He chooses—I know He answered. I'm excited about some of the things he's telling me to do.

Frances, pray that God will take my life and make it really count for Him. Unless I can win souls for Him, there's really no purpose in life. I'm really excited about what has happened inside.

I also tried your husband's plan today. I had to compile figures for an emergency pass for the computer. While they stood waiting for me, I started to get panicky, then remembered and said, "Lord, help me put all these figures in this adding machine correctly the first time." When I totaled—it balanced. Just for fun I measured my tape—it was 23 feet long! That's a lot of numbers and I never would have balanced it the first time if God hadn't done it!

Another letter which came from a real old man thrilled me.

Read both of your books (*God Is Fabulous* and *Hot Line to Heaven*) and enjoyed them very much.

Just have to give witness to an answered prayer. You know I have had trouble to swallow at times not too bad, but this last Monday and Tuesday it was so bad I couldn't even get water down.

So Tuesday Eve God and I had a God talk. I told God I had been praying for two days and still can't swallow, NOW I WANT IMMEDIATE HEALING!

Now what do you think happened? My throat opened up and I was OK. Went right out to the ice box and drank two glasses of water—no trouble. Had to go over to neighbors right away and tell them. So now you know that you are not the only one that God answers prayers for. Ha! Ha!

Another letter came recently with a picture enclosed of a real darling teenage girl and boy. After I had spoken at a Christian woman's club luncheon, a mother frantically grabbed me and described her problem to me—her daughter didn't have a date for a very special school affair. We prayed right on the spot for a date for her daughter. This is what the letter said:

When I came home and told my daughter, she replied that you should have saved your breath—because the only boy she would want to go with didn't have any money and wouldn't be calling her.

I prayed hard that God would really reveal to her the power of prayer—and, of course, He did. Several nights later, The Boy called! She has been amazed ever since that it worked out the way it did. Proof again that God really is fabulous.

You Can't Outgive God!

As a speaker, I had never had the opportunity of asking for money at a main service, but I have sat and cringed many times as I have heard pastors apologetically ask for an offering. All I can think of is that everything I have belongs to God, and came from Him and can go back to Him if He wants it, and I appreciate the fact that He allows me to keep enough to live on.

I shall be eternally grateful that the Lord gave me a husband who feels exactly the same as I do, and my heart cries for those people who have not learned the thrill of returning God's money to Him. And then all of a sudden—*it happened!* I was asked to speak for a Christ Birthday Offering. I was so excited I could hardly contain myself—finally to be able to share with thousands of people why I feel people should give generously every time the offering plate comes around. I almost burst, and then the moment finally came!

I don't know when I ever had more fun speaking than I did the day I had the fabulous opportunity of challenging people about their money. It was thrilling. At the close when I asked them to put in their minds the amount they had decided to give to the offering, I then flatly said, "Now, *double* it!" (Everyone thought I was going to ask for one additional dollar, but I fooled them and asked them to double it.)

God's word says "Give and it shall be given unto you, pressed down, shaken down, running all over the place" (paraphrased) and if you're not willing to accept that statement on faith, then you're calling God a liar and I stand firm on what I believe and know to be a fact.

Before I became a Christian we had an expression —"Put your money where your mouth is"—and I decided that statement also applies to a Christian speaker who asks for money, and the Lord had laid upon my heart to return my entire honorarium check. Just as the service started, a long distance call came in from my husband, and I told him what the Lord had laid on my heart, and God's Holy Spirit so enveloped him across the miles, he began to cry, and said, "Honey, you know you don't have to ask me—when God tells you to do it, *do it!*" And so I endorsed my entire check and as I put it in the offering I said, "Jesus Christ gave his *all* for me, so I think it's little enough that I be willing to give *all* of this check back to Him."

Well, we really had fun—I really "hung loose with Jesus" and told them to stop playing the funeral dirge tunes they normally play during an offertory and to start playing some joyous music like "It is Joy Unspeakable"—because God loves a cheerful giver!

The money got counted, and before I left to catch my plane they had collected the largest amount ever collected on the Christ Offering—not only was it larger, it was almost four times the largest amount ever collected! I just said "Praise the Lord" that they had listened as God spoke to them.

I thought no more about this because I came home for just a half day and then left to go on to my next

convention. After about two days at the next convention they asked me my traveling expenses, honorarium, and so forth. Because I was combining two
conventions on one trip and they were not using me
in the evening, I had been booked into other
churches, so I told them that reimbursement for my
expenses would be adequate, and I would make up
the honorarium at the other churches.

I received my check as I left the convention. Usually
I do not look at the check until I either deposit
it en route or deposit it when I get home. When I
opened this check to make the deposit, I was astound-
ed to discover that the amount was exactly *double*
what I had asked! I was so excited I called home to
tell my husband about it, and he said, "Honey, what
did you ask them to give in Oklahoma? Wasn't it double?" I realized then, that because God means it when
he says "Give, and it shall be given unto you" that he
had given me back *twice* what I had asked. And just
for the record, the extra amount I was given was 25
dollars more than I had given in my entire honorarium previously.

Well, there it is, proof again that you can't outgive
God.

For Each Day's Problems

I really love the Living New Testament which Ken
Taylor gave 14 years of his life to translate. This
makes the Bible come alive for anyone who will dare
to read it. So many times, individuals have said to me,
"I just don't think God wants to be bothered with the
little details—He expects us to do them ourselves."
Well, I just can't agree with you on that, because the
Bible says to me that God wants us totally dependent
upon Him at all times. From the LNT I'd like to read
you one little verse: "And now just as you trusted
Christ to save you, trust Him, too, *for each day's*

problems; live in vital union with Him." God doesn't just say the big overwhelming things, but for each day's problems. Here was an interesting situation in our house:

When Charles and I were married, he acquired a lot of things right off the bat: First a wife, then a daughter, then a son and daughter-in-law, a grandson, and heaven only knows what else. Along with Charles, I acquired two old lady cats. Prissy and Tuffy were really huge old girls and had been spoiled tremendously over the years by Charles. However, even though they were pretty ornaments around the house, they became a problem, because Charles began traveling with me, and each time we left town to go on tour, we had to put the cats in a cat hotel.

Now, whether or not you realize it, keeping cats in a cat hotel is an expensive proposition. And every time we came home and got the cats out, when Charles wrote out the check, which usually ran about 50 dollars, I'd look at the cats and my mind would think of other things. I'd think, "That 50 dollars would buy 2000 Four Spiritual Law Booklets, and 2000 of those could mean 500 souls saved for the Kingdom of God!" And then I'd look at the cats and think, "Are you worth 500 souls?" And even though they were nice old ladies, I'd have to admit that they weren't worth 500 human souls.

As we began traveling more and more together, we had to honestly face the situation of what to do with these two dear old ladies. We didn't feel it was fair to them to keep them penned up half the time in a hotel which was quite different from the freedom they knew at home and in the yard, and yet we didn't know the answer, so we prayed and asked God to find a home for them.

Now, there are people who wouldn't believe that God has time for silly little requests like this, but I believe with my heart and soul that God cares about everything we do, and He's always standing there with His loving arms outstretched just waiting for us to reach out and touch Him in prayer. Charles and I were leaving in about three weeks for another trip, so we asked God to find a good home for our little old ladies before we left town on the next trip. Charles asked me if I was going to put an ad in the Houston newspaper, but I said, "No, I asked God to find them a home, and I'm sure that He will," so we didn't insert ads in the local newspapers.

It's one thing to give away little kittens, because everyone likes them, they're so playful and furry, but to give away two old lady cats is another problem! Try it sometime. We waited, and waited, and waited, and prayed and prayed and prayed. Finally it was Friday night before we were to leave on Saturday morning. We had run out of Cat Crunchies, were down to the last can of cat food, and had bought no more at the store.

We ate supper and after supper we were sitting in the living room for a few minutes contemplating what we should do. A friend had called and suggested that we put the cats to sleep as a humane thing to do, but after talking to our daughter who was counseling in a youth camp at the time, we decided against it because she very bluntly said, "Mother, you wouldn't *murder* them, would you?" Charles and I began to pray, "Lord, you know we're such chickens we couldn't have those cats put to sleep, so please, Lord, the time is growing short, would you please, please, please find a home for our cats?" And then we said "Thank you, Lord!"

Somehow or other, we both had a great peace, because although we didn't know *how*, we did know that God had heard our prayer. We had just smiled at each other, with that beautiful assurance that comes from knowing that God has heard, when the silence was broken by the sound of the telephone. Charles flew to the phone, answered it the way we always answer the telephone—"Good evening, God is fabulous" —but before he got back, I was already on my feet heading for the garage to get the cat beds, etc. He caught me in the kitchen and yelled, "Praise the Lord!"

When he had answered the telephone he was advised that some people had wanted a cat for six years and wanted to know if they could come over in 30 minutes and pick them up!

Why don't you try God some time on some of these little things?

CHAPTER 4

TRANSFORMED—BY GRACE DIVINE

"Do not be conformed to this world, but be transformed by the renewal of your mind, that you may prove what is the will of God, what is good and acceptable and perfect."

(ROMANS 12:2, RSV)

RECENTLY I SPOKE at a banquet where the tables were decorated in a most unusual way. On every table there was a big black ugly worm about 12 inches long —very repulsive-looking, with rhinestone eyes and hot pink feelers, and right alongside of it was a beautiful big butterfly, made of multicolored tissue paper. The program that night was called "A Transformed Life" because that's exactly what Jesus Christ did to me.

He transformed my entire life, my reason for living, my reason for being, my purpose in life—well, just my everything! I often wonder if the reason there are so few transformations is because of a verse in Galatians: "Am I now seeking the favor of men, or of God? Or am I trying to please men? If I were still pleasing men, *I should not be a servant of Christ* (Galatians 1:10)." For some reason or other, we are obsessed with the idea that we care what other people think about us, but we certainly can't care what God thinks about us.

Good old Paul, who dared to say, "I'm a fool for Christ's sake, whose fool are you?" He cared what God thought, not anyone else. Give me Christians who care what God thinks, and not what people think.

When I think of a transformed life, I cannot help but think of my darling husband's life, because his story is like so many other people who sit in churches today. Charles was probably as good a moral man as you'd ever find anywhere. He was a devoted husband, a strict and conscientious church man who never missed a church service, never missed a board meeting, was faithful in doing all the works of the church, was the treasurer of a church for approximately 10 years, kept the records up to the minute at all times, gave his money, sang in the choir and was regarded as a pillar in the church.

However, Charles freely admits he was living the "Christian life *on his own.* He was trying to do all the good things a Christian was supposed to do, but the real joy of a transformed life was just not there. He had gone to the altar as a young man and made a decision for Christ, and then the following year had gone for "sanctification" although he didn't even know what that meant, but he knew that he was supposed to have been sanctified, whatever that meant.

For 30 years he continued in this pattern of serving

the *church*, but then the drawing power of God became evident in his life and he felt a need for more and more and more of God, but like so many people he really didn't know what to do about it. Early one morning at a men's prayer meeting where they had coffee and chatter, Charles felt completely engulfed by the Spirit of God, and without any of the usual things which encourage us to make decisions, Charles knelt at an altar in a church and very simply asked God to take "all" of his life and make it spiritually what He wanted it to be.

Charles no longer cared what any man thought about him, he cared what God thought about him, and a desire for the old-time religion of Christ's disciples became the focal point of his life, and his life was transformed. Charles, who used to be the "quiet" one, all of a sudden became filled with God's Holy Spirit and Christ became a *person* instead of a *thing*, and Christ came alive in his life!

All of a sudden Charles discovered he *had* to talk about Christ to everyone he met. He discovered that the average church member doesn't know Jesus Christ personally, and he became overwhelmed by the necessity of sharing Christ with everyone he meets, in business or otherwise. Many people have often felt you can't combine "religion" with business, but somehow or other, since Christ transformed his life, Charles shares Christ and the miracles of daily living with everyone he meets. He no longer is "conformed" to this world, but he has been transformed by the renewal of his mind.

So often we go through life doing all the church "things" but not knowing Christ personally, and oftentimes we do this just because we don't realize how simple it is just to ask God's forgiveness, and then ask Christ to come into our life and take complete control. All I can say is don't pray it if you don't mean it, be-

cause you had better be ready for all the excitement
that God has for you if you're willing to be transformed.

One of the funniest incidents in Charles' life shows
an attitude that is present in almost all of us. He had
been asking God to reveal any attitudes that were not
correct and to "clean them out" of his life. He had
been visiting up in Abilene, Texas, and wanted to get
back to Houston before dark, but he had been sharing
the reality of Christ in his life with so many people
that he got a late start home, and since he wanted to
get as close to Houston as he could before dark, he set
the car on 80 miles per hour and just floated down the
expressway between Dallas and Houston.

He kept his eye on the rear view mirror to make
sure that no police were after him, and was just following the Bible verse which says "Watch and pray"—he
was watching the road and the rear view mirror and
praying that the police wouldn't see him. After a while
he went over a hill and saw all kinds of red lights and
he knew he (along with a lot of other cars) had been
caught by radar, so he pulled over to the side, and he
said the nicest state patrolman you could ever imagine
asked to see his license, which he produced, and then
the policeman told him he was going to have to book
him for going 80 miles an hour on a 70 miles an hour
highway.

Charles impulsively said, *"Eighty* miles an hour?"
just like he was shocked at the idea and would
never even consider going that fast. And then God's
Holy Spirit got after him and he realized that not only
had he knowingly broken the law because he had set
the car right on 80, but now he was going to lie about
it!

He promptly confessed to God and to the patrolman that he was guilty, has paid his fine and has
learned his lesson. Again, P.T.L. for the ability of

God's Holy Spirit to work and convict us of our wrong doings.

We have a little gadget on our car which we set according to the speed limit of the highway or street we're on, and when you go one mile over the speed limit, a most irritating buzzer sounds and doesn't go off until you drop down below the speed limit again. The first time I heard this I asked Charles what it was, and he said, "That's our 'sin buzzer'!" It's amazing what that does to you! The minute we hear that sound, off the foot goes from the accelerator until we're back down within the law again.

One day as we were riding along, Charles and I ventured the thought: "Wouldn't it be a terrific thing if each Christian had a little 'sin buzzer' attached to him?" Just imagine when we think we're so holy and pious how that little buzzer could remind us of even the slightest little infringement. And can you imagine what a church would sound like on Sunday morning? Clang . . . clang . . . clang . . . And yet God's Holy Spirit is the best sin buzzer I know of, if we're only willing to listen to Him, because *this* sin buzzer is the thing that transforms a life.

CHAPTER 5

FEET, TOO?

At a state youth convention where I was privileged to be the speaker, I was advised after I had arrived that the youth had read in the Bible about foot washing, and wanted to have a foot washing service and would I give them a hand. My heart thrilled. They really asked the right person, because of all the ordinances, this one is to me the ordinance of love where

God's great and mighty love spills all over everyone who participates.

During the first service at the convention I wanted to impress the young people that there was more to a youth convention than squirting shaving cream all over the place and that if they really wanted to go home with something other than black and blue marks from pillow fights, they'd just have to hang in there with me and we'd see what the Lord would have us do about a real fabulous convention.

I've discovered so many times young people have a lot of hang-ups and hidden sins that they are reluctant to discuss even with a pastor or counselor, and yet somehow or other they've got to get them out in front of themselves, so that they can all be seen by them and they can ask God for forgiveness. We started the first service by asking everyone to write down on a piece of paper whatever it was that kept them from being a Christian or whatever sin it was that kept them from being the kind of Christian they wanted to be.

I encouraged them to write to their heart's content and I assured them no one was going to see what they wrote because at the end of the service we were going to let everyone burn what they had written. Then I very simply gave my testimony and shared how a personal relationship with Jesus Christ had changed my entire life.

When I had finished speaking I asked each one of them to prayerfully file up to the front, set their "God block" on fire, drop it into the container and ask God to forgive them and remove it by the end of the youth convention. How seriously they filed by, dropping so many slips in that the fire didn't burn fast enough, and we almost smoked the place out before we finally took the bucket outside to burn the "God blocks" all the way down. I wish you could have seen the faces of the young people as they actually gave to God what was keeping them from the abundant Christian life. And what relief they felt in their own hearts having actually seen the problem down on paper.

The next morning we were supposed to have a class in soul winning, or how to lead someone else to Christ, because this is what the disciples did all the time in their old-time religion. They didn't sit around in beautiful church buildings listening to someone preach—they did their preaching out on the streets and the highways and byways and came together in a "church" to share the excitement of what they had been doing. As we used the Four Spiritual Law booklets (Campus Crusade for Christ) and we came to the decision time, I told each of them that I wanted them to make their decision on an intellectual basis. I had shared with them how Christ had transformed my life because I had been willing to remove the "ego" or "self" from my life and just plain give it to Him to live through me.

I've often said the only thing the Lord wants out of us is a "warm body and a big mouth" to share the Good News along the way, and as I explained the loneliness of sin and the excitement of Christ, I asked them just to simply choose which way they wanted to go in life. It's really so simple to be a Christian. Many times in churches they make it so confusing it's impossible to understand at all what it means to be "born again," but it's just a question of asking God's forgiveness and asking Christ to live His life through you.

I had asked a young man on the front row to come up and be my "guinea pig" for the morning session. He briefly resisted as I asked him to come up front, but I jokingly told him this was going to be the most exciting morning of his life, and somehow or other, God's Holy Spirit communicated to him, and he came up and "pretended" to be a "real" sinner while I read the Four Spiritual Laws.

After I had read the verses to him, explaining how God loves him on a very personal basis, and then reminding him of the fact that "all have sinned and come short of the glory of God," I got to the Personal Invitation of Christ where He speaks in Revelation 3:20—"Behold I stand at the door and knock; if any one hears My voice and opens the door, I will come in to him."

And then I told him that "receiving" Christ involves a turning around—in other words, turning to God from self, trusting Christ to come into our lives, to forgive our sins and make us what he wants us to be. I explained it isn't a question of simply agreeing or giving intellectual assent to his claims, and certainly it isn't just having an emotional experience, but a turning over of one's life to Christ.

The easiest way to explain it, I think, is to realize that what we need is to quit saying "I want to do this," I want to do that," "I, I, I, I, I," and turn our thoughts Godward and say, "Lord, what wilt *thou* have me to do?" It really comes down to saying either "God is much smarter than I am" or "I'm much smarter than God and can run my own life." I often wonder how many times in my own life I thought I was more capable than God of running my own life, and I wonder how many times I have messed it up before I recognized and admitted that God was much smarter than I.

What a power-packed moment as I stood there and saw a young man actually confronted with the person of Jesus Christ! The spirit of God was so strong, it was a magnificent thing to be a part of.

I very simply asked him if he would like to pray right then and ask Christ to come into his life. The actual moment of confrontation and decision was a startling thing, because all of a sudden a young man realized that everyone at one time or other has to "do" something with Christ—we either have to accept him as being who he said he was and be willing to let him live through us, or we have to reject him. This young man's eyes opened wide in amazement as Christ confronted him personally, and he made his decision for him as he stood there in front of the entire youth convention.

Young people accepted Christ all over the youth convention that morning, because God had used the "guinea pig" to confront all the other young people there with Jesus Christ.

So many times we feel a decision to accept Christ is all there is to it. Well, that's all there is to the beginning step—but where do we go from there? Do we stop right there, or do we continue with Christ? Too many people stop right there and never go on to reap the rewards of full surrender, so at the evening service that night I spoke on "Where do we go from the altar—back to the pew and back to sinning, or do we go ahead with Christ?"

Really, it's just a question of being obedient to God. If we will get into the scriptures we'll discover that God requires obedience if we want to enjoy that exciting life he promises us. One of the requirements in the Bible is the observation of God's ordinances. For each of the three ordinances, the Lord has given me a very unique experience, so I shared them with the young people, and I'd like to share them with you.

The first thing that came up in my Christian life was the matter of communion. The first Sunday I went to a church after God had spoken to me in a hospital was Communion Sunday. The pastor had said it was open communion to all Christians, so I sashayed right up there knowing well that I was a Christian and so I could participate in communion.

It's a good thing the Lord forgives a sinner, because I was as big a sinner as anyone could ever have been when I took communion that particular Sunday morning.

When I finally learned what a Christian was and that I certainly was *not* a Christian at that time, I asked God to forgive me for partaking of the communion when I was not a child of God. The Lord's Supper is reserved for those who believe in the "old-time religion" that Jesus saves and those who believe the statement he made: "I am the bread of life; he who comes to me shall not hunger, and he who believes in me shall never thirst." Communion has always meant a lot to me since I became a Christian instead of a counterfeit Christian, because it's a rare privilege and honor accorded to real Christians.

God dealt with me next on the subject of baptism, and even though I had been "sprinkled" when I was a youngster, God's Holy Spirit so dealt with me that I was baptized by immersion when I was 49 years old. And what a glorious day that was! I had been arguing with God for many weeks on the subject of baptism (see *God Is Fabulous*) and when I was finally obedient to Him and submitted to this ordinance, something very special happened in my life and I have never been the same.

I found Christ in a church which believes and practices foot washing, and when the first Eastertime rolled around I remember seeing a little item in the church news about a "foot washing" service. I was talking to the pastor a little later on and said, "I never heard of anything like that—but surely in this day and age you don't actually wash feet, do you?" I was horrified and repulsed by the idea. His only comment was, "Come and see!"

Well, I was absolutely confident that there wasn't any denomination in the entire world that did any-

thing as old-fashioned as foot washing, but nevertheless I continued to question him about it and his only
answer was "Come and see." I was convinced that it
was a symbolic thing and that he would explain the
meaning of it, but I still wasn't convinced about
going, and I kept talking to God and praying to God
and asking Him to reveal to me in a very definite
manner what I should do about this area in my life.

I continued talking to the pastor because I had 13
spiritual children by this time and like most spiritual
children are in the beginning, they were all hanging
on to their "mother's" apron strings, waiting to see
what momentous decision I would make toward this
particular ordinance. We had all been baptized together, so they were anxiously awaiting word as to
what "we" were going to do regarding the foot washing service. I knew I only wanted to do what God
wanted me to do, and God's Holy Spirit was doing
such a marvelous job of convincing me that I finally
half-heartedly said I wouldn't mind washing someone
else's feet, but NO ONE was GOING TO WASH MY
FEET. And that was that! I still kept trying to find out
what the service was all about, but the pastor still very
firmly said, "Come and see!"

On Maundy Thursday when the service was to be
held, my pastor came into the office to bring some
printing, and I started laughing again because I was
so positive that this was so old-fashioned that absolutely no one in this day and age would participate in
such an antiquated custom. Even my pastor got the
giggles at my fantastic interest and yet my refusal to
go along with what the Bible says.

A friend of mine had just accepted Christ and I had
started out giving each one of my spiritual children a
Bible (then I went broke) and she had mentioned
that she wanted one exactly like mine, so I went to
the store to buy her one and opened it at random just

to check and make sure the printing was exactly like mine, and would you like to know where the Bible opened up? To the 13th Chapter of John—and it seemed to me that one sentence literally jumped out at me. "If I do not wash you, YOU HAVE NO PART IN ME." My heart sank—but there was nothing I could do but obey. I said, "O.K., Lord, I get the message, I'll go," because all I could think of was *my* refusal to let someone wash my feet.

I called my spiritual children who were waiting at my house for dinner and to see what the decision was going to be about the foot washing service that night. I told them God had spoken to me in no uncertain terms so I was going, and I thought it would be fabulous if they all wanted to participate, too. I raced home from work so I could be at the service on time, and the sight that greeted my eyes was as hysterical as anything I've ever seen. Lined up on my patio in the back yard were all the pots and pans I owned along with basins, buckets, and so forth. Each one was filled with the highly chlorinated water from the swimming pool and each of the kids had their feet soaking to make sure they were clean for the service that night.

Clippers, nail files, emery boards, scissors were all over the place, because everyone wanted to make sure their feet were pedicured just right for the service. We still knew that *maybe* only one person would actually participate, but they still didn't want to take any chances. At the dinner table I read to them the following:

Jesus, knowing that the Father had given all things into his hands, and that he had come from God and was going to God, rose from supper, laid aside his garments, and girded himself with a towel. Then he poured water into a basin, and began to wash the disciples' feet, and to wipe them with the towel with which he was girded. He came to Simon Peter; and Peter said to him, "Lord, do you wash my feet?" Jesus answered him, "What I am doing you do not know now, but afterward you will understand." Peter said to him, "You shall never wash my feet." Jesus answered him, "If I do not wash you, you will have no part in me."

All of us left and went to church together.

The church was softly lit with candles and there was a very special awareness of God's Holy Spirit. The organ was softly playing and everyone was sitting quietly in his seat. We all took our places and after a brief talk by the pastor, he explained that the foot-washing service was strictly voluntary, and all the men who wanted to participate would go to the room on the right and the women to the left, where preparations had been made.

I went to the left and for one brief moment when I walked into another candle-lighted room I almost panicked, because the basins and the large barrel of water said this was the "real thing." But God's Holy Spirit completely enveloped me as I heard someone start singing "Oh, How I Love Jesus." We silently filed around the room and each sat where he chose. The women in charge were girded with long towels (just like in the Bible) and since they had neither shoes nor stockings on, they asked us to remove ours.

I sat in utter amazement as two of the women picked up a basin apiece, filled it with water from the barrel, and knelt down in front of two other women, and proceeded to cup their hands with water and run the water over the feet of the woman they had chosen. After each foot was treated the same way, they were dried and the kneeling woman rose from her knees and hugged her sister in Christ whose feet she had just washed.

Never have I been so privileged to feel the power of God's Holy Love as that night. How could you ever hate anyone who washed your feet, and how could you ever hate anyone whose feet you had washed? It's an impossibility. Then the long towel was removed from the waist of the first woman and presented to the one whose feet she had washed, and she in turn refilled the basin and went to the next woman to wash her feet.

The service went around the circle and I was one of the last ones because of where I was sitting. Because I was obedient to God in submitting to this ordinance, God granted a blessing far greater than I deserved—the one who washed my feet was my best friend (the alcoholic in the book *God Is Fabulous*) who had washed my feet many times in years past when I had been bedridden for many months. So there was nothing but great love as she washed my feet, since God knew this was my stumbling block and in my being submissive to Him, He made it easy for me.

Then I in turn washed the tiny feet of the wife of my beloved pastor, and love flowed between the two of us like a great rushing river. God's mighty love when we allow it to be unleashed is the most powerful thing in the entire world. Never will I forget the night or the experience.

As I shared the above with the young people at the youth convention, I then challenged them with a question: "Where are you going—forward or backward?" Then they were told that they, too, could participate in a foot washing service that very night under the stars, on a strictly voluntary basis. Even though they were given the choice of ping pong and other sports, 90 percent of them selected the foot washing service. They silently filed outside and the boys went to one side of the mountain, and the girls to the other where preparations had been made. The first ones were selected to start and the service began.

The stars were twinkling in a midnight blue sky and there was a holy hush all around the place. Softly we heard the boys begin singing "Oh, How I Love Jesus" and then the girls picked up the echo and sang it back. Pretty soon many of the other beautiful choruses and well-known songs were sung, and people began standing up telling what the service had meant to them. The testimony time went on for over an hour and love flowed over the mountains in a never-ending stream as these young people, most of them for the first time, participated in this beautiful service.

I might add that my favorite saying of "Praise the Lord and pass the Kleenex" was really apropos that night because as we rejoiced and basked in God's love, the tears flowed freely. The young people over and over said this was the highlight of the convention as we said goodbye! One really sharp on-fire Christian girl of about 17 said to me, "I never believed in this emotional stuff, but that foot washing really got me last night." Give me the kind of religion where we let the Spirit of God really move on our young people.

Communion the following morning really was a perfect climax to the convention because we all assembled on the top of the mountain and read from the 22nd chapter of Luke, then gave them assignments to read in Matthew, Mark and 1 Cor. Each one was challenged to read these scriptures, meditate upon them, and then to be still and listen to God. As God spoke to each heart, they were to go down to the edge of the lake where the communion table had been set and to partake of communion. Never has there been such solemnity and purpose as these young people participated in another ordinance. Once again was felt the mighty power of God in dealing with the lives of these young people. Many of them said that since they had been obedient to God it was the most wonderful weekend of their lives because they had really seen God!

CHAPTER 6

EVEN TODAY!

David and Goliath

It's AMAZING how the answer to every problem in life is revealed in the Bible, if we will just believe. Over and over I hear people talk about the Bible being old fashioned, and we have to update it, and we have to be more liberal and understand that times are different today than they were when the Bible was written! But somehow or other, I feel that God wrote it as something timeless, and so it's just as effective and relevant today as it was when it was written.

Every once in a while I run into an interesting situation when I speak. I'm thinking of a youth convention I went to where because of a lack of supervision, teenagers had run rampant, doing a lot of damage, and the spiritual quality of the convention was a real big zero. My part was limited to the time that had been allotted to me, but nevertheless I felt an urgency to bring the gospel undiluted and without compromise to them. I was discouraged when I heard of some of the pranks of the senior high and college youth the night before. They had poured honey inside clothing, and all sorts of non-Christian pranks had been pulled.

Don't misunderstand me, I certainly approve of the

young people having a marvelous time, and I think their energy can be well expended in sports activities and the like, but it doesn't have to be used up doing things which fail to glorify God.

I really prayed as I sat in my cabin, asking God to reveal some way that I could make them realize the relevancy of the gospel. Somehow or other, the Bible opened to the story of David and Goliath. Now, when you think of the story of David and Goliath, what do you think of? Almost everyone thinks of one of two things. They think of a little guy who killed a giant. Or they think of a slingshot and five shiny little stones. I suppose I had always thought of this story as the little guy who had killed a giant, but since this was apparently what God wanted me to read, I reread the story asking God to reveal the special message he had for me.

Read the 17th Chapter of I Samuel—but let me point out a few interesting little things. "And David said to Saul, 'Let no man's heart fail because of him; your servant will go and fight with this Philistine.' And Saul said to David, 'You are not able to go against this Philistine to fight with him; for *you are but a youth*, and he has been a man of war from his youth.' . . . 'Your servant has killed both lions and bears; and this uncircumcised Philistine shall be like one of them, seeing he has defied the armies of the living God.' And David said, 'The Lord who delivered me from the paw of the lion and the jaw of the bear, will deliver me from the hand of this Philistine.'"

Read on a little more and then visualize tiny, little David. He put on a helmet of bronze and a coat of mail and then put on a sword over the armor, and he was so weighted down he couldn't even move. I have often seen children playing out in the vacant lots with makeshift swords tied around their waists, and falling over the clothes and shoes they were wearing which were too big for them, and I can picture just what little David looked like. Finally David took them off and said "I can't go with these, for I am not used to them." So instead he chose five smooth stones from the brook and put them in his wallet, picked up his sling shot and drew near to the Philistine.

Now I really like this next part of the scripture. "And the Philistine came on and drew near to David, and his shield-bearer in front of him. And when the Philistine looked, and saw David, he disdained him; [I think he laughed out loud] for he was but a youth, ruddy and comely in appearance. And the Philistine said to David, 'Am I a dog, that you come to me with sticks?' And the Philistine cursed David by his gods. The Philistine said to David, 'Come to me, and I will give your flesh to the birds of the air and to the beasts of the field.' "

You know, this coming from a giant would scare even the mightiest of men, but not little David. Think of the courage involved as David said to the Philistine, " 'You come to me with a sword and with a spear and with a javelin; but I COME TO YOU IN THE NAME OF THE LORD OF HOSTS, the God of the armies of Israel, whom you have defied. This day the Lord will deliver you into my hand, and I will *strike you down, and cut off your head;* and I will give the dead bodies of the host of the Philistines this day to the birds of the air and to the wild beasts of the earth; that all the earth may know that there is a God in Israel, and that all this assembly may know that the Lord saves not with sword and spear; FOR THE BATTLE IS THE LORD'S and he will give you into our hand."

Those were pretty strong words for a little guy, weren't they? But you know the rest of the story—David put his hand in his bag and took out a stone, and slung it, and struck the Philistine on his forehead, and killed him. It was as simple as that, because he had come IN THE NAME OF THE LORD OF HOSTS. This is "hanging loose with Jesus" when we can come in the name of the Lord of Hosts, just as David did. Can't you just see that little guy with only a sling shot telling this huge giant that he was going to strike him down and cut off his head? I can just imagine he had his fist raised in the air as he proclaimed that this was all going to be possible because he came in the name of the Lord of Hosts.

Reading this story at this particular time thrilled my very soul all the way to my toes, because God had spoken to me so vividly saying to me to go in the NAME OF THE LORD OF HOSTS, and slay the dragon, because the BATTLE IS THE LORD'S. I really prayed and said, "Thank you Lord, for never has my plan of action been laid out as plainly as it was that day." I put on the whole armor of God, which was his Holy Word in this case, and went out to the battlefield. I told it "just like it is" because I just didn't believe that Christ would do the things the young people were doing if he were living his life through them. If you've ever been at a youth convention where the old devil really breaks in, you'll know how everything can be against you, but it was amazing how the Spirit of God went to the battle with me that day just like He went with little David because truly, the "battle was the Lord's" and not mine, so I didn't have to do a thing, but "hang loose with Jesus" and say the things he told me to say, and we ended up with a most successful, exciting and *spiritual* youth convention.

I had 49 years of a "social" religion—just give me that "old-time" religion where we depend on God and His holy word and upon the power of His Holy Spirit.

Ananias and Sapphira

God hasn't changed one single bit, and neither has Christ, since the happenings in the Bible. The world has changed a lot, and the people have changed their way of doing things, but the message of the Bible can never change. Often when reading a story in the Bible, a present-day application comes to mind, and I'm going to share this little story with you, not because it was thought of by me, but it's a thought my husband shared with me, and with which I concur wholeheartedly.

The average Christian lives a half-hearted relationship with Jesus Christ. We become so bogged down with the things of the world and with all the little details of life that we have less and less time to do the things that God has called us to do. As a matter of fact, take your own church. Go and call up every "member" in your church and ask them to come out to a soul-winning program, or a dinner or any activity of the church and see what your response is. Tell them it's very vital for them to be present for seven straight nights of a revival service and see how many excuses you can get.

Now, these will all be from very "dedicated" Christians who will feel that their life is so wholly dedicated to God and that they are such good Christians, they just "know" you will understand why they can't make it this particular time, and yet each time you call them the excuse is the same.

Think of the story of Ananias and Sapphira (4th chapter of Acts—32nd verse on—Again I am reading from the Phillips translation*). If you remember the story, "The apostles continued to give their witness to the resurrection of the Lord Jesus with great force, and a wonderful spirit of generosity pervaded the

---

*The New Testament in Modern English, J. B. Phillips, Copyright © 1958 by The Macmillan Company, New York.

whole fellowship. Indeed, there was not a single person in need among them, for those who owned land or property would sell it and bring the proceeds of the sales and place it at the apostles' feet. They distributed to each one according to his need. It was at this time that Barnabas sold his farm and put the proceeds at the apostles' disposal.

But there was a man named Ananias who, with his wife Sapphira, had sold a piece of property but, with her full knowledge, reserved part of the price for himself. (He had a little larceny in his soul.) He brought the remainder to put at the apostles' disposal. But Peter said to him,

"Ananias, why has Satan so filled your mind that you could cheat the Holy Spirit and keep back for yourself part of the price of the land? Before the land was sold it was yours, and after the sale the disposal of the price you received was entirely in your hands, wasn't it? Then whatever made you think of such a thing as this? You have not lied to men, but to God!"

As soon as Ananias heard these words he collapsed and died. All who were within earshot were appalled at this incident. The young men got to their feet and after wrapping his body carried him out and buried him.

Shortly after this Sapphira came and Peter asked her to verify the price the land was sold for and she also lied, and when Peter told her they had buried her husband and they would bury her also, she collapsed at Peter's feet and died.

Now think about this parallel to modern-day living. We are willing to give a part of our life to Christ, a part of our time, a part of our thoughts, and a part of our money, but somehow or other, that little bit of larceny in our hearts makes us lie and fib about why we can't get to church, why we can't go out on the soul-winning program, why we can't "afford" to give our money to the Lord, and lots of other things. Many times we hold for ourselves a love for something or somebody a little higher than our love of God—another god before God!

Do you think this story could apply to modern-day living in that like Ananias and Sapphira we are willing to give only part of our lives and are holding back the rest for ourselves? That on that great day of judgment when the Lord brings forth from our memory bank all of the things that ever happened to us in life, he will count us dead spiritually because we have held back that little bit of self and have refused to give him all? I believe with my heart and soul that many people will be very surprised and disappointed to discover when they get to heaven and cry "Abba, Father" that God will say "I know you not." And only because we have held back that little portion of self which we cannot find time or the desire to give to Him who gave His all for us.

The Bible very plainly states that you cannot serve two masters at one time, and any part of you that is not controlled by God is controlled by Satan as was that little part of Ananias and Sapphira. Therefore since you can't serve both at the same time, if the devil has even the slightest little foothold, I wonder how many will be carried out dead spiritually because of this withholding attitude? The devil isn't particularly interested in having full control of us, all he wants is a tiny little bit of us, for God's Holy Spirit cannot live in the same temple occupied by Satan.

Think of the joy that was had by those men who gave their all for Jesus Christ, and compare it to the discomfort that Ananias and Sapphira must have had when they knowingly lied to the Lord. Could this be the reason for so many unhappy and defeated Christians today? Give me people who "hang loose with Jesus" and give their all, and let God have His way!

Jesus Christ Is the Boss

It's amazing how God will reveal the necessary things to you right now from the Bible if you just believe. Recently in our home we had a woman come to visit us who was discouraged about her spiritual life. I had talked to her for a while, then felt a nudge from God's Holy Spirit to call my husband in, so he began to share and to attempt to nail down what the spiritual problem was. She continued to talk about "churches" and we kept talking about Christ, and finally my husband asked her point blank if she had ever actually asked God to forgive her sins and Christ to come into her life. She answered that she had gone to church all her life, but that she had never done just that, so after explaining to her this was the problem in her spiritual life, she prayed and was born again right in our Texas room.

Shortly after this she began talking about her resentment against her boss and how she felt she was being demoted because her job had been changed and she felt it was a low blow, etc., and she was saying all kinds of unflattering things about her boss. Charles said she should do her very best on the new job and say "Praise the Lord, give thanks for all things" and to put her whole heart and soul into her new job.

While my husband was talking, I "happened" to pick up a copy of the Phillips Translation and it flipped open to The Letter to Colossae and something really jumped out at me, and so I read out loud to this woman, "Whatever you do, put your whole heart and soul into it, as into work done for the Lord, and not merely for men—knowing that your real reward, a heavenly one, will come from the Lord, since YOU ARE ACTUALLY EMPLOYED BY THE LORD CHRIST, and not just by your earthly master."

That's a fabulous thought—"You are actually employed by the Lord Christ!" (Colossians 3:23-24). If we all really believed that, just think what would happen to our world economy today. People would begin honestly giving their best to their employers, and as a result, there would be far more efficiency in offices, factories, homes, and so forth, production would be at a higher rate than ever before, employer-employee relations would be at an all-time high—and, well, I just can't go on any more than this because it would be unbelievable what would happen if we honestly felt that we were employed by Jesus Christ. But also think how exciting it would be, and think of the progress that could be made in all areas if we honestly believed it.

And it's amazing how the Lord puts these little scripture gems before you if you are willing to take time to read his word. I left two days later on a tour and when I arrived at my airport destination I was given a note which advised me I was to go to another airline and buy a ticket for later on in the week to a town I had never heard of. Since I never know who's going to meet me, I always follow instructions, so I went over to the other airline and as I stood there I mused, "I wonder what I'm going to be doing in ———?"

The airline clerk looked at me and said, "You must travel for one of the big companies, because I notice that a lot of them send women around the country these days." Then he asked me the *big* question. He said, "Who are you employed by?" I very simply said "Jesus Christ!" . . . I wish you could have heard him laugh. You could hear it throughout the entire airport it was so loud. But it's amazing when you go in the power of God how things like this don't bother you, so I just stood there until he finished laughing, then he looked at me and said, "You're serious, aren't you?" And I said, "You'd better believe I'm serious, because Jesus Christ *is* my boss."

Then I began to share a little of my story with him and before long he was asking if he could get another fellow there to listen to the story, too, because, "He really needs to hear this too—he's been divorced four times already."

It always thrills me so to see how God's Holy Spirit can encompass any situation as long as we are willing and able to respond and do what He calls us to do. And do you see how God had put into the memory bank of my mind just the right words when I was asked by whom I was employed?

Same Boss

On a recent trip my husband joined me and then we came home together. When we arrived in Houston, we were exhausted from an extremely rigorous schedule; we came in at an odd hour, there wasn't anyone to bring our car to us, so we took a cab home. Personally I felt like collapsing after the long plane ride, but when we got in the cab, knowing full well we had prayed that the Lord would prepare a heart for us, my husband started sharing the fact that it was a wonderful day because of our boss. Naturally, the cab driver wanted to know who our "boss" was, and so we replied "Jesus Christ!"

This really shocked him, so he wanted to know more. What church did we represent, and things like that. We told him we didn't represent any particular denomination but simply the man Jesus Christ, the only one who could forgive a man of his sins and could promise him eternal life. We shared how Christ had redeemed us (each one of us have a very different story to share) and then we asked him about his personal relationship with Jesus Christ.

His answer inspired us, because he told us that he had accepted Christ several years ago, and the Lord had spoken to him so vividly that he had attended a

Bible college in Texas for two years, and then made the statement that so many people make: "I just couldn't live the Christian life, so I went back into sin!"

We told him naturally he couldn't live the Christian life, because no human being can, but that if he would fully surrender his life so that he could say as Paul said, "I have been crucified with Christ, therefore it is no longer I who lives, but Christ who lives within me, and the life I now live in the flesh I live by faith in the Son of God, who loved me and gave himself for me," he would discover how exciting the Christian life really was.

He was still suspicious and wanted to know what church we wanted him to join, and we said "none" because our sole purpose is to win people to the Lord and then return them to their own churches or to suggest any good Bible preaching church which honors Christ. We talked on and he revealed how he had been out drinking the night before and had woke up in the morning feeling so "dirty," as he expressed himself, and full of guilt, and he said he had promised the Lord that he was going to "get right with Him" before the day was over.

To show you how the Lord was working, he had waited for more than two hours at the airport for a fare and was getting so discouraged when "all of a sudden" we happened to come along. Charles advised him that *this day* he had an appointment with God because we had prayed and asked God to send us someone to share the Good News with, and the Lord had kept him waiting until our plane arrived and put us in his cab.

He still wasn't convinced because he had to get rid of a lot of "things" in his life before he could become a Christian, but by the time we drove up in our driveway some 25 miles from the airport, he very emotion-

ally said, "Let's pray!" And so we did, and he asked
Christ to come into his heart and he asked God to
forgive his sins and to really take control of his life
and to live his life through him. It was as though the
sun broke through the clouds as his face lit up after he
had prayed.

This is "hanging loose with Jesus" or obeying God's
slightest command just like the disciples did when
they took the message to everyone they met. Robert
has called us many times since we got home, advising
us of his progress and setbacks as he takes his own
life back again, and we've assured him this happens
to many people, but he's excited about what Christ is
going to do in his life!

CHAPTER 7

I BELIEVE!

"Lord, I believe; help thou mine unbelief."

—KING JAMES

"I believe; help my unbelief."

—R.S.V.

"I do believe, help me to believe more."

—PHILLIPS

"I DO have faith, oh help me to have MORE!"

—LIVING GOSPELS

EACH TIME I read any or all of the above translations
I think of how applicable this is to all of us. Most people today have some kind of a faith—some not so
strong, others stronger—but all of us often find ourselves in a position of crying out to the Lord, "I DO
have faith, oh help me to have MORE!" And it's that

little "more" of faith that somehow or other does the trick.

I could never write about "hanging loose with Jesus" unless I included something about "old time" divine healing. So many people do not believe in the power of God to heal today, but with my heart and soul I believe. And yet even now as I say "I believe" I wonder how many times I have had to cry out "Lord, I believe; help thou mine unbelief," or to put it in more modern language, "Oh help me to have MORE!"

Before I became a Christian I scoffed at "faith healers" because I was positive that God didn't heal people today. I believe that God uses many things, including doctors and medicines, but I also believe that God heals divinely in ways we can never understand.

All I know is what the Bible says and in the 5th Chapter of James, the 13th verse says: "Is any one among you suffering? Let him pray. Is any cheerful? Let him sing praise. Is any among you sick? Let him call for the elders of the church, and let them pray over him, anointing him with oil in the name of the Lord; and the prayer of faith will save the sick man, and the Lord will raise him up; and if he has committed sins, he will be forgiven." I have seen God heal in miraculous ways as this scripture was complied with, and I have also seen God heal without anointing and without the elders gathering around.

My husband is a C.P.A. and is always exceptionally busy around income tax time. And from what he tells me, this is one time of the year when his hay fever hits him the worst. This year, the last Saturday before the tax deadline, he was working at home trying to get so many things done, but he was plagued by one of the worst attacks of hay fever I've ever seen. He sneezed and sneezed; we prayed and prayed and prayed—and he continued to sneeze. I could see how miserable he was getting, and I knew he had some medication which he could take that would relieve him in a few short minutes, so when I saw the torture he was going through, by late afternoon I finally said, "Honey, why don't you take one of those pills this time to get you through the day and then we'll pray the next time you get hay fever again?"

He looked at me as if I had stuck him with a dagger. Even though he said it with love, he emphatically said "No!" I simply cried out to God, "Help thou mine unbelief!" because I felt I had really betrayed God by not believing that He could heal Charles' condition right then.

Satan really came in about this time because Charles began feeling worse and worse and later that day he reached for the medicine bottle in desperation and almost had his hand on it when he said "No!" He prayed again, saying, "God, I don't know what you expect but I'm going to trust You," and within five minutes all signs of hay fever had gone and have not returned at this writing.

I often wonder if this simple act of faith on Charles' part might not have been part of God's plan for my life, because the week following this I left to go to western Pennsylvania to speak to several of the Christian woman's clubs in the Pittsburgh area. There was great excitement in the air as a record number of reservations had been made and the meeting had to be transferred to a night club room to be able to hold all of those who were coming. On the way up to Pittsburgh the night before I was aware of the fact that I didn't feel as good as I usually do. I didn't think it was anything serious, so I ignored the symptoms.

I had a fair night, still didn't realize what was the matter with me, but by the next morning I was on the miserable side of life suffering with cystitis. Anyone who has ever had this knows how painful it is. I got dressed and went to the Christian woman's club and the pain got worse and worse, and in my panic-stricken state I thought "I've got to call Charles—I've got to go home—I've got to call a doctor—I've got to get to a doctor"—And then finally, and last of all: "I've got to pray!"

Now I wonder why that had to come at the very end? I went to the rest room, knowing full well that in less than 20 minutes I was due to speak to the women sitting out there, and almost blacked out from the intense pain. At that moment I realized there wasn't time to call Charles—there wasn't time to go home—there wasn't time to call a doctor—there wasn't time to get to a doctor—in desperation I realized the only thing there was time for was prayer, the thing which I had left to the very end, and in agony that almost tore my soul apart I silently screamed the one word "God" and nothing else.

I was backed into a corner and there wasn't anyone or anything else I could call on except God and I think at the exact same moment that God heard my cry he dramatically touched my body and instantly the pain and the problem was gone. I straightened up and stood there and said, "Thank you, Lord, help thou mine unbelief." I realized that had there been time, I would have tried all of the other things first, but in my complete desperation I had to be totally dependent on Him and He heard my cry.

That night I stayed at the home of a Christian doctor and his wife and I was sharing with them what happened at the CWC, and he said, "Frances, the only thing that could have happened today was the divine hand of God Himself, because there is no medication known to science today that can heal cystitis in less than three days, and yet there I saw a perfect specimen of health with no aches, no pains, no problems. To God be the glory, great things He has done!"

And how God used these two experiences to create a third is another exciting story. I had called Charles at night and related to him what had happened and how God had dramatically healed me. The following day was the final day of the tax season, and one of the women in his office came and told him she was going to have to go home because she was so sick. Then Charles related to her how God had touched him and then had delivered me from my problem and she said to him as she started back to her office, "Will you pray for me?" Charles answered, "Well, let's pray right *now!*" They prayed, and then Charles was called to spend some time with a client, and 30 minutes later when the client left, the woman came in and said, "I'm healed—I don't have to go home after all!"

"Call on Me, and I will show you great and mighty things!"

I never fail to get excited over the way God answers prayer. Sometimes it seems fervent prayer is so necessary before God hears and answers, and then sometimes the most simple little prayers will bring dramatic results!

After I had returned home from a long hard trip, I had a day and a half at home to get ready for another trip, and as I sat at my desk trying to get caught up on some of my correspondence, I kept feeling a tremendous tiredness—my legs ached, and my eyes felt like burned holes in a blanket, I had a headache but I continued working to the best of my ability, feeling confident of the fact that after another good night's sleep I would be in good shape for the trip.

I continued to feel more and more tired, and by the time I sat down to dinner, I could hardly eat, and in the middle of dinner, I said to my husband, "Honey, I'm so tired, I've got to go to bed!" And when I get up and leave my supper, you know there's something wrong!

I went right to bed and when he came to bed, he put his arms around me and instead of asking me how I felt, he said, "Honey, *you're sick!*" I was shocked because it had been many years since I had been sick, and I said, "I am?" And he said, "You're burning up with fever—no wonder your legs hurt, and no wonder your eyes feel like they're burned holes!" I said, "Charles, get me some aspirin, *quick!* I can't be sick, because I've got to catch the early plane in the morning for Oklahoma." Charles didn't move, or release his hold on me, but very softly he said, "Honey, wouldn't you rather pray?"

God's Holy Spirit really spoke to me, and I'm so glad that God uses my beloved husband's words to convict me when I'm wrong, and I said, "Sure, honey!"

Charles lovingly prayed this simple little prayer in which he asked for five things. He said, "Lord, she's your girl, so please touch her body and take away the fever and make her well, take away the pain in her legs, her headache, give her a good night's sleep so she'll wake up completely refreshed, and then, Lord, will you put a protective shield around her so she won't feel the heat as she goes to Oklahoma?" Then he simply said, "Thank you, Lord, for protecting your girl."

I might have struggled for just one short second, but then it seemed as if God had just covered me with a protective coating, and I remember nothing else, but Charles told me this is what happened: Within just a few seconds my forehead had broken out with sweat, but before this happened, I had completely relaxed and was sound asleep. Then the sweat disappeared, and in less than a minute my forehead was as cool as could be because the fever was gone! I slept until 2:30 in the morning and when I woke up I told

Charles I felt like I could have gotten up and tangled with tigers and come out the victor.

So many times we just fail to call on God *first*, and he's right there with his loving arms outstretched, just waiting to take care of us and protect us.

You might wonder what happened to the fifth request my husband made—for my protection from the heat. He asked this because I had been in Oklahoma two weeks earlier, and the intense heat had almost made me physically ill. The daytime temperature was running around 114 and the night wasn't much better. When I got to Oklahoma the next day, the temperature was 109 and it stayed there and above during my time there.

On Sunday afternoon I was standing out in the sun with another evangelist, and everyone was perspiring —the men's shirts were soaked down their backs—and someone said to me, "How come you're not perspiring at all?" I merely replied, "My husband prayed and asked God to shield me from the heat." The other evangelist turned to me and said, "Did you pray that too?" It was so amazing to see the two of us standing there (he even had his coat on) with no signs of discomfort or a sign of perspiration because we had both asked God to shield us. Even though our prayers were the same, they were sent up to God 1500 miles apart and yet God answered them both.

May I say at this point that I do not understand divine healing at all. I only know that God does heal in a miraculous way today, if we will just ask. I don't really know the requirements of asking, whether *we* must have faith, or whether someone else must have faith for us, or whether it depends on the degree of faith we have, or what.

I especially enjoy reading the 8th and 9th chapters of Matthew where Jesus does a lot of divine healing, and in each instance while there is a similarity, there is also a difference. When the leper came before him he said, "Lord, if you will, you can make me clean." And he stretched out his hand and touched him, saying, "I will; be clean." And immediately the man's leprosy was cleansed. In this case the leper didn't know if Jesus wanted to heal him, but he believed if he wanted to that he could!

The next few verses deal with the centurion who came to him in behalf of his servant saying, "But only say the word, and my servant will be healed." And then Jesus said, "Go; be it done for you as you have believed!" This time it was not the faith of the servant, but the faith of the centurion.

Then Jesus saw Peter's mother-in-law lying sick with a fever, and with no one asking him, "he touched her hand, and the fever left her." Whose faith was involved here?

The next verse deals with the fact that "they brought to him many who were possessed with demons; and he cast out the spirits with a word, and healed all who were sick." And, whose faith was responsible in this case? Then in the 28th verse, two demoniacs met him, coming out of the tombs, and the demons begged him, "If you cast us out, send us away into the herd of swine." And Jesus simply said "Go." And you know the rest of the story—the whole herd rushed down the steep bank into the sea and perished in the waters. Who had faith here? The demons? The 9th chapter starts off with a paralytic who had been brought to Jesus by his friends and after discussing the subject of sin, he then said to the paralytic, "Rise, take up your bed and go home."

Well, I don't know the answer—because in each of the above instances, there is a different point to be brought out. But in each of them, the person involved was healed, so I take divine healing with a belief that we should ask, and "the prayer of faith will heal the

sick," and if for some reason or other God doesn't answer my prayer, then I should pray, "Lord, I believe,
help me to believe *more*." Old fashioned? Maybe, but
it's good enough for me.

CHAPTER 8

NOT I, BUT CHRIST

ONE OF THE most unusual experiences of my entire
life occurred when I had an opportunity to speak at a
convention in June of 1969.

It all began like this. I had been at the same convention the year before autographing copies of my
first book, *God Is Fabulous*, and had been real excited
about being able to attend a large international religious convention (my first). I heard some inspired
sermons, but somehow or other, I felt that something
was missing in the campmeeting.

I felt led to pray upon returning home, and this is
what I prayed—I simply said: "Lord, they don't need
to sit there and hear 18 sermons during the week. The
lay people can hear sermons at home from their own
pastor. What they need is something *new*—something
to give them enthusiasm so they can return home *excited* about Jesus Christ, not with sermons to lull them
into complacency about what good Christians they are.
So, Lord, may I please have the opportunity of sharing
the *excitement* I feel about Jesus Christ in that great
auditorium so they'll wake up and go and tell the
world the story of Jesus Christ?" I concluded with a
"thank you" and then that prayer was recorded in the
memory bank of my mind.

I probably was the least surprised person in the
world when I received a letter stating that the com-

mittee was inviting me to speak on Thursday afternoon at 2:45 P.M. on the subject "Ways of Witnessing"
—for the very simple reason that I had asked God to
let me share my excitement about Jesus Christ, and
certainly the reason I stay excited all the time is because I constantly witness as to the *now* power of
God in daily living. There was probably nothing else
in the letter that was earthshaking only some details
to be followed, and that was all.

I immediately wrote back with great joy as follows:
"My first reaction to speaking in that tremendous auditorium was violent stomach pains, but then I remembered that God has never called me to do anything that He hasn't given me the ability to do, so it is
with great excitement and anticipation that I accept
the privilege of sharing the excitement I feel in witnessing for Christ and in seeing souls won for the
army of Jesus Christ."

I had been on many speaking engagements from
the time I received the letter until convention time,
sharing the blessings of God. Just before the convention I received a memorandum telling what each
speaker was going to talk about and after my name
was a little notation, "I *think* she has chosen for her
subject, 'Go, Man, Go!'"

This was interesting, because somehow or other,
God has never led me to write out word for word in
advance what I'm going to share, regardless of where
I speak. I learned early in my Christian life that God
did not call me to be a preacher, but instead just
called me to enthuse people, so my talking is constantly sharing the things that Christ does in my life.

I may have even tried to prepare some kind of a message for this *big* event, but couldn't, and yet somehow
or other, I knew that God would give me the right
words at just the right time. (Please remember since I
only share what I have *seen* and *heard;* it is easy for

me to recall). I think it's interesting that everything we have ever seen, heard, felt, smelled or touched is stored in a computerlike memory bank of our mind and can be recalled at any time (not necessarily as *we* will it, but as *God* wills it).

I was excited about such a fabulous opportunity to share with people my ideas about "giving Christ away" and had no nervousness or apprehension (so I thought). The morning of my talk I got into the auditorium early and went up to the huge pulpit, which seemed about 20 feet above the ground, and looked out into the vast auditorium. I stepped back and then went back up there again and nearly fainted! It was huge!

I thought, "I'll never be able to do it!" Then I remembered the verse I had chosen. "I have been crucified with Christ; it is no longer I who live, but Christ who lives in me; and the life I now live in the flesh I live by faith in the Son of God, who loved me and gave himself for me." If I really believed this, how could I possibly be afraid, when it is Christ who is living his life through me. My usual exuberance returned and I spent the rest of the morning in a witnessing conference and then I ran over to my room to change clothes for the big event!

Maybe someone reading this book doesn't believe in the devil or the powers of Satan. Believe me, I do, because just about the time I got into the suit I had planned to wear, Satan started bombarding me. He said, "Who do you think *you* are, to get up in front of all those people and try and speak? What do you think you can say that will change their lives? You're just a layman. You're not a theologian or anything of the sort. Just wait until you see what a flop you're going to make of yourself." I could almost hear the fiendish laughter of Satan himself as he tried to put fear into my heart.

Something happened, and for the first time in my entire speaking life, I broke down and cried. I not only cried—I sobbed and sobbed as my whole body was convulsed with fear. I wanted to run as fast as I could—just anything to get away from that mammoth auditorium which looked like a huge mouth about to swallow me up. Then I remembered "I will *never* leave you, nor forsake you." (Heb. 13:5)

A cool breeze began blowing in the window and I felt like I was bathed in God's Holy Spirit, and two things happened simultaneously: A tremendous peace flooded my soul as I simply said, "God, with the power of your great and mighty Holy Spirit, I bind the hands of Satan, and claim victory for you this very day."

I didn't ask God to let me deliver the most powerful message or the greatest sermon or anything of the sort, but I very simply prayed with every fiber of my being and every ounce of sincerity I have in my body, "Lord, may your Holy Spirit walk in that great auditorium as He has never walked before." I blotted my tears, slipped into my shoes and walked directly to the auditorium. I wondered at that time if part of the letter to Ephesus wasn't written just for me in that year.

From the Phillips Translation, 1:15 it says (and I think of Paul talking directly to me): "Since, then, I heard of this faith of yours in the Lord Jesus and the practical way in which you are expressing it toward fellow Christians, I thank God continually for you and I never give up praying for you; and this is my prayer. That God, the God of our Lord Jesus Christ and the all-glorious Father will give you spiritual wisdom and the insight to know more of Him; that you may receive that inner illumination of the spirit which will make you realize how great is the hope to which He is calling you—the magnificence and splendor of the inheritance promised to Christians—*and how tremendous is the power available to us who believe in God. That power is the same divine energy which was demonstrated in Christ when he raised him from the dead* and gave him the place of supreme honor in Heaven."

Fear was gone because "perfect love castest out fear" and I was like a race horse running to the wire. All restraint was gone and there was nothing holding me back, and as I got up to speak, a most unusual feeling overcame me. Somehow or other, even though I was in a huge pulpit elevated high above the auditorium, I felt like I was sitting down on the stage, watching this person who had the same kind of white suit I had on, talk with absolute assurance about the things which God had done in her life.

As she shared story after story of different witnessing escapades, I knew somehow or other that they were mine—that they were things that had happened to me, and yet I sat right there listening to a voice which sounded just like mine spewing words out so fast I could hardly hear at times. I felt a tremendous urge to pray for this woman who looked like me, and sounded like me, because there was such an urgency in her voice, I wanted to ask God to make sure that she said everything that should be said, and then all of a sudden "I" was standing there.

I looked at my watch as this other woman was still talking and realized that my time was gone. My prayers, my dreams of God's Holy Spirit moving in a day-of-pentecost way, hinged on what this woman had said, and I realized that I had to listen to what "man" had said, because I must conclude by a certain time. I wondered, "Did God really hear my prayer this afternoon as I asked that His Holy Spirit walk in that auditorium as He had never walked before?" But I knew there was no more time. All the words that needed to be said were either said, or must now be left unsaid. Time had run out.

Emotionally I was drained, even though I felt like I had not been talking during the entire time, and I felt like crying, so I laid my head down on the pulpit and cried out, "God, hear my cry!" I don't even remember what I prayed because I was so overcome by the power of God that nothing seemed to matter. When I finished praying, I lifted my head, and the beautiful strains of "Kum Ba Ya" softly but completely enveloped the huge auditorium. Come by here, Lord! And come He did!

As I stood there it seemed to me everyone was getting up to go to conferences in groups of 50 at a time, and I wondered what had happened that so many people had to leave early to go to conferences, and then I got the shock of my life, because I realized they were not leaving, but responding to the power of God's Holy Spirit, and coming forward. The prayer rooms were filled in just a matter of seconds, and my pastor—who was sitting on the platform with me—stopped them from going in, and asked the people to stand in front of the huge platform.

For one brief moment, I believed that Satan tried his last fling because I might have thought "Wow, am I good!" but God cracked me right in the back of my knees and quietly but firmly said "Who did it, you or me?" I stepped back down from the pulpit, and never went up again because I knew that God had answered my prayer, but that nothing was to my personal credit. I remember looking out at all the people whom God had touched—and I especially remember an old Negro standing there, with tears streaming down her face, but looking right up to Gloryland saying "Thank you, sir, thank you, sir!"

Praise the Lord that His Holy Spirit can work today

to move people just like it did on the day of pentecost!

There's an interesting incident that was the result of this! Many people came on the huge platform to shake hands with me, many pastors asked me to come and share my excitement in their congregations, and many apologetically said, "I'd love to have you, but I know you're too busy to come" and all I could think of was "ye have not, because ye ask not" and "Help thou my unbelief," "Ask and ye shall receive," but I smiled and said nothing. When the line finally dwindled down, a young girl who was obviously pregnant had been sitting on the sidelines weeping her heart out, and then she came up and said, "My people *need* you, my people *need* you, you've got to say you'll come! Please, please, please," she pleaded. Then she added, "We can't pay you, because we don't have any money, and our congregation is small, but my people *need* you, will you come?"

Never have I heard such eloquent pleading, never have I ever heard such a concern for people as I heard in this young voice, and never have I felt called to any church like I felt called to this one. I merely said, "Yes, I'll come. You go home and write me a letter telling me that you're the little girl with the big tears, and I'll come to your church. I don't know how or when, but don't worry about the money, because I *know* that God will provide my every need." I don't know why, but I thought of the widow's mite—I thought of a little church that couldn't offer transportation, or anything else, but offered all they had—an invitation from a sincere heart.

I went home from the convention, and even though I got an almost immediate letter from Hill City, Kansas, telling me it was from the "little girl with the big tears," I first got a letter from Ft. Collins, Colorado, asking me to visit that city for a few days. This was immediately followed by a letter from Augusta, Kansas, asking me to be the speaker at a Christian education convention the week following when I was to be in Colorado.

If you have a map, I wish you'd look at it real closely. You may not even be able to see Hill City on it, because it's a very small town and doesn't appear on many maps, but if it's on yours, you can draw a line from Ft. Collins to Augusta, and right in the middle of that line you'll find Hill City. A little girl with big faith, and she wasn't afraid to ask. Give me people who believe that God will answer prayers today and who believe the Bible when it says: "Ask and ye shall receive!" I checked the year book which lists the membership of this particular church as 30, and yet the faith of the pastor's wife gave her courage to know that "nothing is impossible to God."

CHAPTER 9

"HE'S NOT ON THE PROGRAM"

I'VE JUST GOT to share with you an incident which indicates very clearly what I mean by "hang loose with Jesus"—in other words, listen to what God says and then obey him *instantly*.

On a tour the Lord made it possible for my husband to join me midway, and he was to meet me at a church where the pastor firmly believed that there could never be any deviation from the "program." While waiting for my husband to arrive, I spoke at an afternoon service, and I had told them that if during the middle of the service I saw my husband coming in they'd better just "hang loose with Jesus" because I was going to run down the aisle and plant a big kiss on him.

Well, the afternoon service continued and concluded, and my husband's plane and pony express trip hadn't delivered him yet, so we went to a scheduled tea, and just as they started pouring, someone at the end of the fellowship hall yelled, "Frances, hang loose with Jesus!" I knew this meant that Charles had arrived, so I ran as fast as I could down the fellowship hall, and when Charles heard this expression, he took off at a run and we met half-way in the fellowship hall and he really planted a *big big* kiss right on me.

I want you to know we were "hanging loose with Jesus" because we knew that God had wanted him there, and I also want you to know that because we were not concerned with what people thought, but what God thought, our love communicated in such an exciting way that we got a standing ovation for that kiss. We'll probably never get another one, but that one was exciting.

I told the pastor that since my husband was with me, I felt led to share our most unusual love story that night, but he insisted that it "wasn't on the program" and so we couldn't do it. He was insistent that nothing in the program could be changed, so there was no room for my husband, and yet I have seen what the sharing of our story has done to churches all across America, so I asked God again, and the answer came back the same—share your story.

The pastor insisted all through supper that Charles couldn't speak with me that night because it "wasn't on the program" so I told the pastor to "hang loose with Jesus" and he said that wasn't on the program either, so we went right on. When the service started and my husband walked up with me, he even commented that we were coming together but that I was the only one to speak, and he even refused to call me by my married name, but I just smiled inside and said, "Lord, you'd better talk to him." Then my husband and I went up together and shared our exciting love story, which God uses in a most unique way.

All during the service the pastor was shaking his head and talking to his wife telling her this couldn't be done because "it wasn't on the program" and I'm sure that if Christ had returned to the earth that night, he would have told him he couldn't do it because "it wasn't on the program." When we finished speaking, more than two-thirds of the congregation came forward to rededicate their lives to Christ, and the pastor was still saying, "You can't do it—it's not on the program."

You'll probably think I'm a real rebel to go against a set program. I am not, believe me, but I also feel there's room for change if God is really doing the leading and if we're really "hanging loose with Jesus." I often think of church programs on Sunday morning where we have the invocation, sing a song, have the choir sing a song, read some scripture, sing another song, have the pastor prayer, have the announcements, take up the offering, sing another song, have the sermon, sing an invitation song, have the benediction and then go home not having been inspired the least little bit.

I love services where people are willing to listen to what God has to say—because there isn't any place in the Bible where it says we have to have all these little formalities. Many times I have gone into churches and asked them to sing something lively instead of some old dragging slow song which would put even the most energetic person to sleep, and I've even been known to just tear up the program when God was leading in another direction.

I just think of all the "goodie" things that God has for us out there if we'll just learn to "turn loose" and be willing to listen to what he has to say to us. I *often think of a church* I went to, which hadn't changed one line of the program for 25 years. Apparently I must have really jarred them, because the next Sunday the minister distributed the Sunday bulletin which read as follows: On the Morning Worship side it said "same old stuff" and on the Evening Worship side it said "Same old junk." Across the front of the bulletin he had written to the pianist, "George—hang loose with Jesus." He sent me a copy of the bulletin with a notation that it was the most exciting service he'd ever had in his 20 years in the ministry.

God speaks to us many times, but we ignore the nudging of the Holy Spirit because we're concerned with what people will think of us. All I can think of is that if "you shall know the truth and the truth shall set you free," why get all bound up with what people will think? Life is so exciting when we are willing to just let God have his way and in spite of everything you might think, God's way is always best even though sometimes we might wonder, but never have I seen God's way anything other than first best! Maybe I should say "hanging loose with Jesus" is really just trusting God.

I often think of what the great, late Henrietta Mears said. "If I had my life to live over, I would just believe God." I changed it a little to say, "If I had my life to live over, I would just trust God for every single little detail of my life." Think what a blessing this can be to you if you just know that from this moment on you could depend on God for everything.

And *you can!* Today we put so much emphasis on achieving instead of believing. It's such an accomplishment to us to brag about how well our children did in school, how well they're doing at the piano, how well they're doing in football, and so on. This is important to their growth and maturity, I know, but how much emphasis do we put on their benefits? How often do we mention as the prime accomplishment of our children the fact that they have accepted Christ?

I am consumed with an uncontrollable passion and desire for the things of God. In our house we put Bible reading and inspirational reading before anything else, including TV, magazines and the like. We have a Bible in easy reach at every telephone, in every bathroom, as a matter of fact, in every room in the house. We read all the new translations and we are all privileged to underline madly at all times. Some of the greatest "fun" times we have are when we get whatever translation we're reading at the time (right now its *Reach Out—the Living New Testament*) and get in bed and just share with each other the little nuggets we find on each of the pages. We don't necessarily read the same part of the Bible, but we keep saying, "Listen to this . . . listen to that."

If you'd just try that it would be the most thrilling thing in the world, because I believe the more we get involved with God's word, the more we can understand what "hanging loose with Jesus" or just trusting God means, because over and over and over I discover all of God's little and big promises for us. I'm sure that eternal life began the day I surrendered *all* of my life to Christ. What he gives on this earth is just a taste of what's coming next, but when I walk through the door which leads from earth to heaven, it will be just more of the same, only better, and so many of us don't avail ourselves of these fabulous promises of God just by trusting Him.

I just love to read God's word because He speaks to me constantly through His word, advising, protecting, chastising, loving, warning, calling, and doing many more things. When my heart was crying out for a closer walk with God, I got into His word. Sometimes we think we don't have time to read the Bible. Why don't you try writing down how each hour of a day was spent? Did you ever take inventory of how you spend your time? Try that for a little experiment and see how much lost time there is in your everyday schedule.

Put some of this "lost" time to work for you by reading the Bible. Sometimes I get so tickled at women who tell me that I just don't understand because all I have to do is run around the country talking about Christ and writing books. What they don't realize is that I have to do the same things they do—only I have it a lot more concentratedly than they do, because I have to do it all during the short time I'm at home. But because I have so little time I've learned to do things double time, or to do more than one thing at a time.

God talks to you and to me through His Holy Word. How can we talk to God? By prayer, of course. I've been so excited with the unbelievable number of letters which I have received since I wrote *Hot Line to Heaven* from people telling me it has revolutionized their prayer life. We ought to pray more. *Nothing* brings me into a closer relationship with God than just putting my needs, my hopes, my desires before Him, and trusting Him to take care of all of them.

If somehow or other we could just sneak time to talk to God while we're washing dishes, while we're driving the car, while we're cleaning the house, while we're doing the ironing or while we're cutting the grass or pruning the shrubbery and doing any number of myriad tasks, it could turn the world upside down.

I think dishwashing time is a marvelous time to learn a scripture for the day. Or even ironing can be fabulous if you're learning a verse. Try ironing and as you're banging the iron down on the board keep memorizing, "I can do all things through Christ which strengtheneth me!" and you'll be amazed at how quickly the ironing flies by. I keep "religious" records on my stereo so I can listen to some songs about God to keep me in tune, and you'd never guess how many times God has talked to me in the most exciting ways while I'm doing the mundane things of life.

I get such a kick out of women who spend hours talking about what they have to do during the day. They go into a big harangue about "I've got to do the washing today, and all the sheets have to be changed, and I wonder what we'll have for supper tonight. I think we'll have spaghetti, that's easy to cook—no, I don't think I'll have that because it's so messy to wash the dishes after spaghetti. I know what I'll do—I'll call up Mary and see what she's going to have for supper and maybe she can give me some ideas. I just get so tired thinking about what to have for supper!"

Then she'll spend hours gossiping to her friend and then wonder where her day went to. I usually just say, "Lord, what shall we have for supper?" and you'd be amazed how he puts the idea into my head instantly. Try it—it really works.

When I go shopping, I do the same thing. Many people delight in spending hours shopping. What a waste of time! I just ask the Lord to show me where the best bargains are and where I can get what I want, and I probably spend less time shopping than anyone else you know.

One time on a trip I ruined two dresses and since I never carry more than five, this really shorted me on clothes. I had one day when I could shop since I didn't have any daytime speaking dates, so I started shopping, and after being completely frustrated at not being able to find anything, I remembered that I had forgotten to pray and ask God to show me the best place to find what I needed.

I prayed, and the pastor's wife, who was driving me around, said, "I know, let's go to ———." We got in the car and went, and within a matter of minutes I had found two dresses my size, half-price (on sale) and just exactly the colors I wanted. See, the Lord knew where I could find them without any more fiddle-faddling on my part. Just try hanging loose with Jesus and being dependent upon God for everything, and see how the miracles pile up in your life.

I hope you notice I'm constantly on the "positive" side of Christianity because of all the fabulous things God does daily in my life. Never have I been surrounded with such great love as I have since I became a Christian. God's love is holding me tight when I go to sleep at night, and when I wake up in the morning God's love is right there reminding me that He has given me another day to be loved by Him and to love in return, and I am reminded of how He has provided an answer to every problem I have encountered since I became a Christian, and how He stands ready to always be there with the solution to any problem which might ever come up in the future.

I often wonder how I ever existed without total dependence on God. I can't imagine any other kind of a life. Even as I sit writing a book, I am so completely engulfed in the power of God's love and His care for me that it's thrilling beyond belief.

I have faced some of the most heartbreaking situations in my life since I became a Christian, and yet the peace promised by God has always been there like a mighty arm holding me up all the time. Never has anything come up that would have completely staggered me in my non-Christian life, that I have not been able to pick myself up from the ashes with a great peace in my heart and the knowledge that God loves me, and if God be with us, who can be against us?

What a marvelous thing to know beyond a shadow of a doubt! Human love is at times variable, but God's love is never anything but the same, constant

ever engulfing love. I think of the things that God has
done for me in the few short years that I've been a
Christian. He has, through the power of His Holy
Spirit, given me a peace which is worth more than
anything in the whole wide world.

Thank you, Lord, for saving my soul.

CHAPTER 10

HOW DO I LEARN?

OVER AND OVER again I'm asked the question "How
can I learn to 'hang loose with Jesus'?" I wish I had a
real simple stock answer to this question. And I also
wish I had a real fast answer to this question, but un-
fortunately, I don't believe there is any pat, fast answer that will transform you into a totally dedicated
Christian. I would like to share with you some of the
ideas and thoughts that God has given to me as I
have searched and sought for a closer walk with the
One who changed my life.

If I were to list the most important thing in my life
which strengthens me and gives me more and more
faith to believe in the power of God, I would say it is
reading the Bible.

I love what the LNT has to say about this in I Peter
2:2: "If you have tasted the Lord's goodness and kind-
ness, *cry for more*, as a baby cries for milk. Eat God's
Word—read it, think about it—and grow strong in
the Lord and be saved."

I don't believe I have ever counseled with any person who complained about the defeat of their Christian life who did not also have to admit that they
were not reading their Bible sufficiently. A starvation
diet of God's Holy Word is the best way to reduce

spiritually that I know of! How can you ever hope to know what God has for you if you don't keep up with his promises?

Recently someone told me that they had heard a comment about me. It went like this: "I don't like her, because she thinks that all she has to do is crook her finger and God will answer her prayer." I don't know who said it, but I'm really grateful that he got the message of my positive attitude.

I wonder if anyone making a statement like that ever read the following: "And I pray that Christ will be more and more at home in your hearts, living within you as you trust in Him. May your roots go down deep into the soil of God's marvelous love; And may you be able to feel and understand, as all God's children should, how long, how wide, how deep, and how high His love really is; and to experience this love for yourselves, though it is so great that you will never see the end of it or fully know or understand it. And so at last you will be filled up with God Himself. Now Glory be to God who by His mighty power at work within us *is able to do far more than we would ever dare to ask or even dream of—infinitely beyond our highest prayers, desires, thoughts, or hopes.*"

Who could ever be negative about a God who promises things like the above. By the way, that was from the 3rd Chapter of Ephesians as translated in the Living New Testament, vs. 17-20.

Why shouldn't I believe that God is able to do far more than I could even ask for? Doesn't His word say so? Why is it we fail to believe what God has promised for us? Recently a minister prayed a prayer that really touched me. As he closed the service where we had seen God move in a mighty way, he prayed, "God, don't ever let her lose her childlike faith." And it struck me that is exactly what I have. I think of my own children when they were small, and how they believed every single word I told them, and I have the same feeling about my Father: I believe every single thing that He says to me—whether it's in His Holy Word or whether it's an answer to prayer, I just believe him with childlike faith. Try it! You can't lose with God.

Read what the Bible has to say about negative thoughts. Anything negative is of the devil! If we would all listen to our conversations, we might discover some interesting things about our attitudes. Did you ever think of the positiveness of Jesus' nature? Think of the time when the disciples were in the boat and the waves were crashing over it. Did Jesus say, "Oh, I'm worried that the boat is going to sink. I'm just positive that these big waves are going to swamp the whole thing, and then we'll all be drowned, and then what will happen to the world." Do you think Jesus said that? I'm sure he didn't, because the Bible tells us that he very "positively" told the sea to be calm. And what happened? The sea became calm. Jesus used his faith in his father in a positive way and claimed what God had promised him, and it happened.

A real good way to think of negativism is to think of some problem area in your life where you prayed and asked God to reveal to you what action you should take. The very first thought that came into your mind was from God, but if you hesitated even for a second, let me assure you that the second thought that came in was from the devil himself. Every time the Lord speaks to one, the devil gets right in there, too, because he's always roaring around trying to devour someone, and how better can he devour you than to put negative thoughts into your mind? There just isn't any better way. Think about this very carefully the next time you pray and see what the second thought that comes into your mind is. Without even knowing what you are praying about, I know the second thought will be a negative one, because this is just how the devil works. So just remember in the future when you are tempted to think negatively to tell the devil to get behind you and flee from him just like the Bible says.

Obedience to God is imperative to find the abundant life. So often God's Holy Spirit nudges me, and I'm sure He does the same thing to you, and these little nudges should be obeyed *instantly*. If you wait for even a moment, the devil's got you with negative thinking telling you it can't be done, or it's stupid or something equally against God.

I think of the times that God had nudged me to speak to someone about the Good News, and many times it has been someone I would be positive would never think of listening as I shared Christ, but as long as I'm obedient to God, it's amazing how God has prepared their heart, and that's why He tells me to talk to them. The devil doesn't want me to talk to them because he knows that God has prepared their heart to listen to me and he trembles in his boots when the Truth is told. I *trust* God, and I believe that He will never let me down, and I do not believe that He will ever tell me to do anything that is not for my best interests.

I like the verse in Galatians 3:11—the last sentence: "The man who finds life will find it through *trusting* God." (LNT) Isn't that beautiful to just know that all we have to do is *trust* God and we'll find life? Think of all the things we've tried to do to find the answer to life, and yet it's so simple—just a question of trusting God (and notice that trusting is a *positive* word).

Can I suggest that you try "thinking to God"? All of us are in the process of "thinking" all the time. When we're alone, we think to ourselves. Remember how many times you've used that expression "I was just thinking to myself . . ." Instead of thinking to yourself, try "thinking to God." This is what we do in our house all the time. All of our thoughts are directed to God. As I write this book, my thoughts are to God, as my husband does his accounting work, his thoughts are to God, as we plan for the future, our thoughts are to God. We don't question what we should do or how we should do it, we say, "God, how do you want us to do that?"

It's amazing how you can center all of your thoughts on God and then you can be sure that your answers are filtered through God. And who could ask for anything better than a life that was totally filtered through God Himself? So many times we will ask 25 outsiders to tell us what to do instead of going right to the source of all answers, God Himself. I like Colossians 2:8-9-10 (LNT) which says, "Don't let others spoil your faith and joy with their philosophies, their wrong and shallow answers built on men's thoughts and ideas, instead of on what Christ has said. For in Christ there is all of God in a human body; SO YOU HAVE EVERYTHING WHEN YOU HAVE CHRIST, and you are filled with God through your union with Christ. He is the highest ruler, with authority over every other power."

Isn't that the most heart-pounding thought when you realize that "you have everything when you have Christ"? How much more could you want? Nothing! Just claim it and rejoice and be glad.

And I really hope that you spend a lot of time in prayer. Some of our greatest and closest moments to God are the times we spend in fervent prayer. I absolutely love to pray. Our entire family loves to pray, because in these moments when we reveal our innermost secrets, thoughts, desires and hopes, God becomes so close to us.

I'm sure that as a family we all love each other

more because of our praying times together. We don't pray memorized words either. Each prayer time is a fresh and invigorating time for all of us. There have been times when for some reason or other I might not have felt on the mountaintop as I would have liked to, and as I've prayed with my husband and listened to his urgency for some situation or other, Christ has lifted me into the very presence of God himself, just as His word promises. "The fervent prayers of a righteous man availeth much," and how true this is.

I was unusually exhausted after a trip I just returned from, and was thinking about *my* problems, and how I had gained weight on the trip, how I was so overly tired, and as I sat there listening to Charles' fervent prayers for some of the people we had counseled with, and for the new converts, all of a sudden my eyes were taken off myself and my problems and were turned toward Christ, who is the problem dissolver. It was amazing how my attitude changed in just a short period of time as I listened and joined with my husband in prayer.

And that little word "attitude" can mean so much in learning how to "hang loose with Jesus." So many times we have wrong attitudes toward our brothers and sisters in Christ. I think of how many times I've heard "I don't know how come *she* gets to sing the solo tonight. She sang it last Sunday, and it's really *my* turn."

How many times have I heard squabbling in churches over who got to do this and who got to do that? How many times have you heard people criticize the Budget Committee, the Music Committee, the Program Committee, the Sunday School Committee, the Youth Committee, and you can just go on down the line. They've really taken their eyes off Christ and put them on problems of people, if you want to express it that way. If we'd only keep our eyes on Christ, our attitudes would improve so much.

Any time you're inclined to criticize, ask God what he would have you do. Ask God if he wants you to criticize. Would Christ "gripe" because someone got to sing the solo two Sundays in a row? Keep your eyes on Christ if you really want to know how to hang loose with Him.

Another exciting way to get on a spiritual bandwagon and stay there is to share your faith with others. I often wonder who gets the most out of my witnessing —the other person who hears and accepts Christ as a result, or me, just because as I hear over and over again the miracles that God has done in my life, it brings me closer and closer to Him and I learn more and more to rely solely on Him for the answer to everything. As I recount some of the experiences in my own life, I am often more amazed six months after a happening than I am at *that* particular time. Right now I'm thinking about the selling of my home in Florida.

I had no idea why, but I did know that God was definite in his instructions, and so I sold the house. My daughter and I lived in a mini-apartment and every once in a while she'd say, "Mother, are you *sure* this is what God wanted us to do?" And then God crossed my path with the man he had chosen to be my husband and my daughter and I moved to Houston. Because I had been obedient to God and trusted him for my future, he knew I had to be rid of the house before I could move. As I have related this story, I am more amazed each time I tell it because of the impossibility of my selling my home, and yet because I did, God continued with His miracles. Tell something to someone today that God did in your life, and see how it refreshes your own Christian experience.

Sometimes we shy away from the word "witnessing" because we think it entails hitting someone on the back and asking, "Why aren't you saved?" That's the world's worst approach, so I hope you never use it. But many times witnessing is just sharing some little tidbit that God has done for you. Think of the stories in this book.

I haven't actually "written" a book. I have just shared with you some of the things that God has done in my life, and it isn't any problem at all, because as I have recounted them on the pages of this book, my heart has thrilled again, remembering the *big* and the *little* things that God does for me. Often people have come up to me after a service and said, "God did the same thing for me!" And I always say, "Have you shared this with others?" And invariably the answer is "No."

You have no idea how people's lives can be touched with a simple statement you might make concerning the miracles of God. I'm often amazed at people listening to my conversations in restaurants, on planes, etc., even though I am not talking directly to them, but they have overheard something that intrigued them about a living Christ, and they have strained their ears to hear the rest of the story. When you go in the power of God, it's amazing how easy it is to share the miracles of God. And if you'll just "hang loose with Jesus" and depend upon God to back you up as you share simple little miracles of faith, it's amazing how God will cause people to stop and want to hear more, more, more!

And I guess one of the points to stress over and over and over is to depend upon the power of God's Holy Spirit. Hanging loose with Jesus is a question of being filled and empowered by the Spirit of God so that you are anointed of God to live your life in Christ. Reread the first chapter on the truth about the disciples until they were filled with God's Holy Spirit, and then call upon this supernatural power for your own life.

I look back at the first book I ever wrote, *God Is Fabulous*, and I think of a statement I made in the final chapter. "I do not know yet what God wants out of my life. I only know that each day I let Him know that I am available for whatever purpose He has for me. And it's a peculiar thing, it doesn't really make any difference what He shows me now that I am waiting on Him, because since I asked Christ to live his life through me, what I do is inconsequential, but I'm really eager to see what he's going to do!"

I didn't realize at that time what I was learning to do, but now I know that I was beginning to "hang loose with Jesus"—to trust him, to obey him, to study his word, to talk about him, to talk to him, to live in the power of his great and mighty Holy Spirit and to know that you "have everything when you have Christ"!